THE REAL
GEORGE ELIOT

THE REAL
GEORGE ELIOT

A biography of the writer, a study of the towns and houses
in which she lived, and an introduction to the readers
she continues to inspire

Lisa Tippings

PEN & SWORD **HISTORY**

AN IMPRINT OF PEN & SWORD BOOKS LTD.
YORKSHIRE – PHILADELPHIA

First published in Great Britain in 2021 by
PEN AND SWORD HISTORY
An imprint of
Pen & Sword Books Ltd
Yorkshire – Philadelphia

ISBN 978 1 52675 454 7

Typeset in Times New Roman 11.5/14 by
SJmagic DESIGN SERVICES, India.
Printed and bound by CPI Group (UK) Ltd, Croydon CR0 4YY

Pen & Sword Books Limited incorporates the imprints of Atlas, Archaeology,
Aviation, Discovery, Family History, Fiction, History, Maritime, Military, Military
Classics, Politics, Select, Transport, True Crime, Air World, Frontline Publishing,
Leo Cooper, Remember When, Seaforth Publishing, The Praetorian Press,
Wharncliffe Local History, Wharncliffe Transport, Wharncliffe True Crime and
White Owl.

For a complete list of Pen & Sword titles please contact
PEN & SWORD BOOKS LIMITED
47 Church Street, Barnsley, South Yorkshire, S70 2AS, England
E-mail: enquiries@pen-and-sword.co.uk
Website: www.pen-and-sword.co.uk

Or
PEN AND SWORD BOOKS
1950 Lawrence Rd, Havertown, PA 19083, USA
E-mail: Uspen-and-sword@casematepublishers.com
Website: www.penandswordbooks.com

Contents

Acknowledgements   vii

Chapter One — In which I first make the acquaintance of George Eliot — 1

Chapter Two — In which I pay my first visit to Nuneaton and follow in the footsteps of George Eliot herself — 4

Chapter Three — In which George Eliot's importance as a writer, an academic, a social and political thinker is considered — 22

Chapter Four — In which George Eliot is born and thrives, and her childhood surroundings leave an indelible mark on her conscience — 35

Chapter Five — In which George Eliot fervently embraces her faith before losing it, plunging her father into despair — 50

Chapter Six — In which George Eliot not only faces loss and grief, but is also given some fine opportunities to travel — 78

Chapter Seven — In which George Eliot finds work with the *Westminster Review*, meets G H Lewes and leaves England — 98

Chapter Eight — In which George Eliot lives, loves and thrives while in exile — 124

Chapter Nine — In which George Eliot's views on the role of women in society are further scrutinised and discussed — 137

Chapter Ten   In which George Eliot is persuaded to begin
her career as a novelist   153

Chapter Eleven   In which George Eliot becomes a mother
figure to three sons, and introduces *The Mill
on the Floss* and *Silas Marner* to the world   172

Chapter Twelve   In which George Eliot writes two more novels,
moves house and suffers further tragedy   176

Chapter Thirteen In which George Eliot writes her masterpiece
and suffers a greater tragedy than ever before   183

Chapter Fourteen In which the world loses one of its
greatest writers   188

Further Reading   192
Index   194

Acknowledgements

As a writer with a passion for the nineteenth century, and as a reader who can think of nothing better than disappearing into the maze-like complexities of the Victorian novel, I feel extremely honoured to have been given the opportunity to write this book. The nineteenth century was an era of great contradictions. On the one hand, the Victorians looked forward with intrepid eagerness to the future, embracing the latest technological advancements with a vigour that we, in the twenty-first century, have come to admire. The Great Exhibition of 1851 became a cultural landmark, introducing the British public and visitors from overseas to novelties such as the steam engine and spices from around the world.

At the same time, however, there were individuals who chose to look backwards, and who preferred society to maintain its patriarchal ties so that women continued to be marginalised. Some nineteenth-century doctors even went so far as to declare that too much study could damage a woman's ovaries, making her of little use as a wife and therefore unmarriageable. In America, Silas Weir Mitchell promoted the 'rest cure', a treatment purported to cure the hysteria of an over-stimulated female through enforced bed rest and a diet rich in fatty foods. It was a treatment the American writer Charlotte Perkins Gilman described in her short story *The Yellow Wallpaper*, where the protagonist is forced by her physician husband to rest, and stay confined to a room papered with ugly yellow wallpaper:

> So I take phosphates or phosphites – whichever it is, and tonics... and am absolutely forbidden to 'work' until I am well again. Personally, I disagree with their ideas. Personally, I believe that congenial work, with excitement and change, would do me good. But what is one to do? I did

write for a while in spite of them; but it does exhaust me a
good deal – having to be so sly about it, or else meet with
heavy opposition.

It is interesting that Charlotte Perkins Gilman highlights the fact that it
is not writing itself women find arduous, but the furtive and secretive
methods they sometimes need to employ when attempting to engage in
the act of writing in the first place.

This might be a clue as to why Mary Ann Evans decided she needed
to take further action if she was going to be able to put all her energy into
writing, unshackled by prejudice and the short-sightedness of certain
members of society. Her strength and determination encouraged her to
take a male pseudonym – George Eliot – ensuring she was free to write
and publish the novels of someone who was unwilling to live by the
narrow parameters and strict moral code that others tried to impose upon
her. I am deeply indebted, therefore, to Pen and Sword for allowing me
to tell her story.

As ever, I am indebted to my parents for introducing me to nineteenth-
century life and for beginning a fascination with Victoriana that has
lasted a lifetime. The seeds of this book were truly sown on those Sunday
evenings, when, after watching the latest BBC costume drama, I would
take myself off to my bedroom, tie my dressing-gown around my waist,
and imagine I was wearing a bustle.

I must also give my love and thanks to my husband Nigel and son
Morgan, without whose patience and understanding this book might
never have been completed. Nigel's photographs have been the addition
to the words my book needed, and I cannot thank him enough for being
my photographer, and sharing this experience with me.

In 2019 we celebrated the 200th anniversary of George Eliot's birth.
The world has changed almost beyond recognition during this time, but
one thing which remains timeless is the power behind her words, and
the truth behind the human condition she so clearly recorded for her
readers. In this, she has become a writer to transcend time and is truly
a mouthpiece for all those who yearn for freedom and the opportunity
to be themselves in a world so often restricted by society's rules and
limitations.

Thanks are also due to the George Eliot Fellowship for their
enthusiasm, the literature they produce, and their wonderfully informative

tour of Nuneaton and its surroundings that I was fortunate enough to go on in the summer of 2019.

NB George Eliot is the pseudonym of Mary Ann Evans (later known as Marian), chosen because Mary Ann believed she would be taken more seriously as a novelist by mid-nineteenth century readers if she was believed to be male. Throughout this book, and to ease any confusion, I have referred to Mary Ann Evans as George Eliot. As this is her pseudonym, I have also followed the traditional rule of never using the writer's surname, and therefore I always refer to her name in full, i.e. George Eliot.

Chapter One

In which I first make the acquaintance of George Eliot

'What do we live for, if it is not to make life less difficult to each other?'

(*Middlemarch*)

For many young people, growing up in the South Wales valleys of the 1970s and 1980s often meant enduring a childhood that was demarcated by ritual and custom. Months, weeks and days were all singled out by habitual routines that passed from one generation to the next. Weekends in particular leant themselves to the moulding and shaping of time's great traditions. The still calm of a Saturday afternoon in winter was invariably shattered by the shrillness of a referee's whistle. Families clung frozen to the side-lines, watching in heavy-lidded coldness as their local rugby team waded through conker-brown mud, bodies coming to life only when a streak of colour trampled, coughed and spluttered towards the slippery grey blur of a try line. The air blasted roars of triumph from the winners and grumbles of denial from the losers, victory and defeat washed away in equal measure by a pint of beer, or half a lemonade for us 'little 'uns'.

Sundays wore an altogether more refined air, time broken only in sporadic bursts by the pungency of lazy-day cooking. Sleepy morning eyes opened to the smell of bacon and sausages frying in the pan, and later, mouths watered in anticipation of gorging on the joints of beef or lamb roasting in the oven. As clock hands tick-tocked past midday meals, parents slouched on the sofa in front of the television, eyes half-open, waiting to watch Henry Fonda or John Wayne defend their patch of land against marauding bandits. This was the cue we children needed to take ourselves reluctantly to Sunday School, a pinch of Mother's spit to flatten our fringe, collection money gripped tightly in our unyielding

1

fists, and with only the thought of luke-warm orange squash and damp Rich Tea biscuits to help quicken the demise of the next hour and a half.

The chanting of The Lord's Prayer and the fumbling of buttons and zips led to hasty goodbyes and the walk home, heads stuffed full of well-intentioned goodness. For my sister and I, this meant running over a hodgepodge of pavements, each daring the other to walk on the cracks, before arriving home to half an hour of play-time. A quick swilling of hands beckoned before sitting down at the kitchen table to a tea of salmon sandwiches made from soldier-straight triangles of bread and my nan's home-made currant cake, all washed down with several cups of strong, black tea.

As daylight dimmed to dusk, a tradition particular to the Tippings family would begin. Dad would settle in his armchair, and the rest of us would gather on the sofa to watch the latest episode of whichever costume drama the BBC had currently commissioned. And so it was that late afternoons came to mark the beginning of my love affair with all things Victorian and my first introduction to George Eliot herself.

Season after season, I hid my face behind a cushion as a mad woman in the attic was revealed to be the cause of Jane Eyre's sense of foreboding; I cried as Little Nell breathed her last; and my heart ached for Florence Dombey, who wanted nothing more than to be loved by her father. But it was Maggie Tulliver, George Eliot's passionate and independent heroine, a young woman ultimately doomed to tragedy, who truly caught my imagination. Portrayed with both sensitivity and power by Pippa Guard in the 1978 adaptation of *The Mill on the Floss*, a few Christmases later brought a special gift in my stocking: a navy-covered hard-backed edition of the novel, published by Collins. With its gossamer-thin pages and tiny print, the book became firstly an object I revered on my bookshelf, and later a novel I loved to read. Propped up against the pillows in bed, straining my eyes either by lamplight at night, or by the first wavy strands of sun to poke through my curtains, I would wallow in the beauty and honesty of George Eliot's tantalising descriptions, both of the characters she created and of the world they inhabited:

> A wide plain, where the broadening Floss hurries on between its green banks to the sea, and the loving tide, rushing to meet it, checks its passage with an impetuous embrace. On this mighty tide the black ships – laden with the fresh-scented fir-planks, with rounded sacks of oil-bearing seed,

or with the dark glitter of coal – are borne along to the town
of St Ogg's, which showed its aged, fluted red roofs and the
broad gables of its wharves between the low wooded hill
and the river-brink, tinging the water with a soft purple hue
under the transient glance of this February sun.

(Chapter One, *The Mill on the Floss*)

Perhaps I should also consider the fact that my literary love affair with George
Eliot has thankfully remained untarnished by academia. Over the course of
the ten years I spent studying for everything from my GCSEs in the 1980s
to my Master's degree in Literature during the early 2000s, I have never once
been called upon to write an essay on a George Eliot novel. Instead, I have
been left free to read and enjoy her works without being quietly consumed
by the fear that someone intends to judge me on my opinion and find me
wanting. I have been able to engage in lively, spirited conversation with
fellow George Eliot enthusiasts in relaxed settings, free from the rigorous,
academic conditions that have overshadowed other literary conversations.
Such freedom has heightened my interest in what draws other readers, from
all backgrounds, both academic and otherwise to George Eliot's novels,
and this has allowed me the time to place a particular focus not just on the
language she has chosen to use, but also on the places that inspired her.
These two subjects, her readers and the places where she lived and wrote,
are topics I have kept coming back to over the years and the results of my
discussions and travels are partly what inspired me to write this book.

My other inspiration takes me back home, and to those Sunday evenings
spent curled up on our old pink velour sofa, sat alongside my sister and
mother, my father in his armchair and the television tuned to BBC 1. Across
the screen, Pippa Guard as Maggie flaunts, sulks, tramples and demands.
As young as I was, Guard's performance helped make clear to me that in
spite of what some history books at school chose to depict, nineteenth-
century women were made of stronger stuff than their implied propensity for
fainting, consumption and gossip suggested. In Maggie Tulliver, Eliot created
a heroine with an appeal that transcends time, and whose independence and
determination could inspire all women, from the flapper to the feminist, from
the teenager on the cusp of womanhood, to the adult looking for solace and
consolation. And if some women hope there is a little of Maggie Tulliver's
impetuosity within them, or they yearn to harbour some of Dorothea Brooke's
compassion and intelligence (*Middlemarch*) or Gwendolen Harleth's wit and
charm (*Daniel Deronda*), who would ever blame them?

Chapter Two

In which I pay my first visit to Nuneaton and follow in the footsteps of George Eliot herself

There is already a great deal of unmapped country
within us which would have to be taken into account in
an explanation of our gusts and storms.
(*Daniel Deronda*)

I make my first ever visit to Nuneaton on a Saturday in early February. It is dark and brutally cold when I leave – the air serrated by sharp pellets of frost which appear to pin-hole the windscreen with smatterings of silver. The scarf that is wrapped halfway around my face concertinas into ripples every time I turn my neck, making vision difficult. But without it I am cold and limpid, rather like a 7-year-old George Eliot must have been when unable to sit near enough to the fireside at Miss Lathom's School for girls. I remind myself that I am a grown woman, push the scarf further down my neck, and prepare to start the car's engine.

Nuneaton

It takes almost three hours to reach Nuneaton from Swansea. I have mapped the journey carefully, placing the postcode of each interesting landmark into my satnav in the hope of avoiding spending precious minutes constantly circling and re-circling the same roundabout. In the nineteenth century, such a journey would have meant taking a small holiday, a coach and four, several stops to rest the horses and at least one night's stay at an inn. It is little wonder many people fail to understand my obsession with life as it was 200 years ago, but then not everyone spends hours dreaming of what it would have been like to alter the course of women's history, to stand strong against a tide of male prejudice, and to shock the backward thinkers with my literary accomplishments, even if I would have enjoyed doing it wearing a blush-pink bustle.

As I drive, I find it easy to become distracted and wonder how north Warwickshire, and the countryside around Nuneaton, might have looked in the early part of the nineteenth century when George Eliot first knew it, and first walked through its streets, fields and lanes. As I travel along the motorway, putting distance between myself and Swansea, each flash of yellow and red reminds me that the convenience of modern living, with its fast food empires like McDonald's and KFC, although lambasted by the healthy eaters, are sometimes all that stands between the busy and insanity. If George Eliot's mother had known of a place where food could be quickly purchased, there is every reason to believe she too might have succumbed to the occasional takeaway, safe in the knowledge that it would keep her growing brood of children both quiet and somewhat nourished. As something of a novice cook myself, I am aware of how often I rely on takeaways, restaurants and microwave meals to give succour to my hungry family. I often ponder on the fact that in spite of my obsession with life as it was almost two centuries ago, I would have been a sore disappointment as a nineteenth-century wife. My tendency to daydream would, I am sure, have kept me long enough away from the kitchen and stove for my husband to reprimand me severely and threaten me with a visit from the local parson, all too eager to admonish me with a sermon on the importance of a woman fulfilling her wifely duties.

As I arrive in Nuneaton, I find that its smallness confuses me. I had been expecting something larger, perhaps even more industrial on the outskirts, and more commercial at the centre. But the town appears medium-sized at best and, despite being declared the largest town in Warwickshire, is welcoming in the way that large towns seldom are. People nod their morning greetings in the same way they do at home in the suburb of Morriston and I realise this is a town well-versed in keeping strangers happy. Having been warned not to be disappointed by the town's lack of historical ephemera, I am also pleasantly surprised by the Victorian red-bricked buildings that skirt along the outer-rim of the shopping area. Alongside the Saturday market and the solid-looking pub, they are a constant reminder of the fact that towns do not spring from nowhere simply for our convenience. Every high street has a shop-owner or customer from another era who will flavour the general history of a place with their own particular story, and their own particular triumph or tragedy. Nuneaton is simply fortunate that George Eliot is the woman to add her own indomitable tale to its otherwise mainly industrial past.

I have already decided that the first stop on my itinerary shall be a visit to George Eliot's statue. Situated in the heart of Newdegate Square, it is easy enough to find, and I am immediately drawn to the facial expression on which the sculptor, John Letts, has chosen to focus. It is at once full of quiet sorrow, a woman captured in quiet, pensive thought. Yet beneath the downcast eyes, there is a hint of something else. Determination? Intellectual steel? The statue was commissioned in 1986, and as with all monuments created long after their subject has died, it is an amalgamation of many years' worth of academic analysis, as well as the sculptor's own personal interpretation. Letts' statue also displays a subtle beauty, something critics and readers have pondered over for years, especially given the somewhat cruel comments and jibes that were often made about George Eliot's personal appearance. As I walk away from Letts' statue, I realise how much I like it. I approve of its subtlety, and the way he has captured in her eyes, even many years after her death, a quality it is easy to believe George Eliot displayed throughout her lifetime: intellectual rigour. I like to think George Eliot herself would have given it her own seal of approval.

The debate about George Eliot's appearance should, of course, be a non sequitur. After all, her appearance matters little to those who enjoy her novels or study her works, and to speculate seems to belittle her academic value to the point where, in true nineteenth-century style, a woman is valued only in so far as her beauty fits the mould of what was appreciated at the time. Furthermore, apart from the odd comment on his eccentric choice of colourful waistcoats, it is hard to find many letters, articles and essays dedicated to the appearance of Charles Dickens, for example. However, when completing any research on George Eliot, it is almost impossible to do so without practically tripping over reams of comments concerning her facial and physical appearance.

Henry James

In a letter to his father, the writer Henry James wrote what is often quite rightly believed to have been one of the most scathing attacks on George Eliot's appearance. Following a meeting in 1869, he commented bluntly:

> She is magnificently ugly – deliciously hideous ... She has a low forehead, a dull grey eye, a vast pendulous nose, a huge mouth full of uneven teeth ... Now in this vast ugliness resides a most powerful beauty which, in a very few minutes steals forth and charms the mind, so that you end as I ended, in falling in love with her ... Yes behold me literally in love with this great horse-faced blue stocking.

The hyperbolic bluntness of James's language is breath-taking, but beneath the brutality of his description, there are undoubted compliments. Her 'ugliness' is 'magnificent,' her 'hideousness' is 'delicious'. More to the point, James admits to having fallen in love with her, because beneath her 'ugliness', he has perceived her 'powerful beauty'. George Eliot was 50 when James first met her. She was regarded as an important novelist and thinker, and after meeting her at her London home, the Priory, James believed he had met a 'counselling angel', and like one of the many important nineteenth-century figures who gathered there to meet with her, he left in awe of her conversational abilities. It is difficult to wonder why her appearance needed to be commented on at all.

Her physical appearance was something George Eliot had been consciously aware of since her youth. In believing her sister Chrissey was favoured by their mother because of her more delicate features, she convinced herself to equate her perceived poor appearance with a lack of attention and love. The truth was probably that the biddable Chrissey was easier to mould and discipline than her infinitely more headstrong sister, but it ensured that the writer was always keenly aware of her need to be loved, and at times she searched for approbation even when her actions meant that was difficult to find. This is a problem a young Maggie Tulliver wrestles with in *The Mill on the Floss* (1860). Maggie's cousin Lucy Deane is praised by Mrs Tulliver for being 'such a good child' with

a row o' curls round her head, an' not a hair out o' place.
It seems hard as my sister Deane should have that pretty
child; I'm sure Lucy takes after me nor my own child does.

Such praise for another young girl, spoken so openly in Maggie's
presence, forces her to throw off her bonnet and shake the 'crop' of
dark black hair that causes her mother so much distress. Later, when all
the aunts and uncles are gathered at the Tullivers', and tired of further
remonstrance regarding the wildness of her hair, Maggie, in a fit of pique,
takes a pair of scissors and hacks off much of it, causing Mrs Tulliver to
cry and declare, 'She's a naughty child as'll break her mother's heart'.

In her youth, George Eliot had known the discomfort that could
be felt by an individual made to feel uncomfortable in their own skin.
She wanted her legacy to be one of honesty and truth, where, within the
maze-like pages of her plots, and beneath their twists and turns, there
was advice to be found and help to add succour to the daily lives of her
readers, irrespective of their appearance.

The Red Lion

It is this thought that takes me to my next landmark, the George Eliot
Hotel on Bridge Street. Once known as a coaching inn called the Bull
Hotel, it became the inspiration for the Red Lion in *Janet's Repentance*
from *Scenes of Clerical Life* (1858). This was the first time the writer
used her pseudonym, and as I stand shivering in the cold outside the pub,
I wonder how often George Eliot may have walked past the Bull Hotel,
and at what moment it seemed like the perfect inspiration for her own
creation. The pub as it stands today is solid and square, and in spite of
the modern signage and boards displaying 'two bottles for five pounds',
and a declaration that it is, 'the home of live sport', the sash windows
and nineteenth-century style of outdoor lighting lend an air of traditional
charm to the building. The pub sign depicts a portrait of George Eliot
as painted by François D'Albert Durade in 1849, when the writer was
30 years old. It is a much softer depiction of her than some descriptions
would lead us to believe could be possible, and perhaps this is why this
particular portrait has been chosen for the sign. A tender bloom of pink
highlights the sitter's cheeks, and she somehow appears younger than

her actual age. Her eyes are soft, an almost dewy dove-grey, and there is certainly nothing about this depiction to suggest that in twenty years' time, the writer would deserve to be labelled as 'magnificently ugly'.

However, much more important to readers of George Eliot's novels, and in particular to readers of *Scenes of Clerical Life*, is the fact that in spite of being on the Isles of Scilly when she wrote *Janet's Repentance*, George Eliot's reminiscences still took her back to her childhood home of Nuneaton, which became Milby; St Nicholas Church, which was renamed Milby Church; and the Bull Inn or the Red Lion, as she described it in her book. It is difficult to dispute the fact that her childhood and the years spent at Griff House had such a huge impact on her, especially as aspects of them appear in various incarnations throughout her literature.

In *Janet's Repentance,* the Red Lion makes an appearance particularly early in the story, and its bar is the setting of one of the religious arguments that sets in motion the main action of the story. When a new curate is appointed to serve the chapel at Paddiford Common, some of the townsfolk are in favour of the newcomer, the Reverend Mr Tryan and welcome his evangelical preaching style. However, the rest of the congregation, headed by the bullish lawyer Mr Dempster, prefer the method of preaching practised by Mr Crewe, the old curate:

> 'No!' said lawyer Dempster, in a loud, rasping, oratorical tone, struggling against chronic huskiness, 'as long as my Maker grants me power of voice and power of intellect, I will take every legal means to resist the introduction of demoralizing methodistical doctrine into this parish; I will not supinely suffer an insult to be inflicted on our venerable pastor, who has given us sound instruction for half a century.'
>
> It was very warm everywhere that evening, but especially in the bar of the Red Lion at Milby, where Mr Dempster was seated mixing his third glass of brandy – and – water. He was a tall and rather massive man, and the front half of his large surface was so well dredged with snuff, that the cat, having inadvertently come near him, had been seized with a severe fit of sneezing – an accident which, being cruelly misunderstood, had caused her to be driven contumeliously from the bar.
>
> (Chapter One, *Janet's Repentance*)

The Red Lion makes another appearance in Chapter Four. This time Mr Dempster has acted upon his words and organised a protest regarding Mr Tryan's employment as curate:

> 'Yes, yes,' said Mr Dempster. 'Keep up a jolly good hurray.' No public duty could have been more easy and agreeable to Mr Powers and his associates, and the chorus swelled all the way to the High street, where, by a mysterious coincidence often observable in these spontaneous 'demonstrations', large placards on long poles were observed to shoot upwards from among the crowd, principally in the direction of Tucker's Lane, where the Green Man was situated. One bore, 'Down with the Tryanites!' another, 'No cant!' another, 'Long live our venerable curate!' and one in still larger letters, 'Sound Church Principles and no Hypocrisy!' But a still more remarkable impromptu was a huge caricature of Mr Tryan in gown and band, with an enormous aureole of yellow hair and up-turned eyes, standing on the pulpit stairs and trying to pull down old Mr Crewe. Groans, yells and hisses – hisses, yells and groans – only stemmed by the appearance of another caricature representing Mr Tryan being pitched head-foremost from the pulpit stairs by a hand which the artist, either from subtilty of intention or want of space, had left unindicated. In the midst of the tremendous cheering that saluted this piece of symbolic art, the chaise had reached the door of the Red Lion, and loud cries of 'Dempster for ever!' with a feebler cheer now and then for Tomlinson and Budd, were presently responded to by the appearance of the public-spirited attorney at the large upper window, where also were visible a little in the background the sleek head of Mr Budd, and the blinking head of Mr Tomlinson.
>
> (Chapter Four, *Janet's Repentance*)

'Public-spirited' he may have been, but George Eliot used the location of the Red Lion to introduce and explore different facets of Mr Dempster's personality. In Chapter One, for example, the lawyer's over-indulgence in snuff and the consequential incident of the sneezing cat may be interpreted humorously. But in reality, Mr Dempster's over-reliance on snuff reflects his addiction to alcohol, and the incident involving the innocent cat being turned out of the pub foreshadows the time later in the story, when Dempster throws his abused wife Janet out of their house.

The abused woman

Janet Dempster allowed George Eliot to explore the character of the abused woman in much the same way as Anne Brontë had done ten years earlier in *The Tenant of Wildfell Hall* (1848) where she discussed the issue of the physical and mental abuse that women could suffer at the hands of their husbands. In *Janet's Repentance*, the reader is presented not just with a woman who is forced to suffer at the hands of her brutal bully of a husband, but also a woman who turns to drinking alcohol in secret as a means of lessening her despair. In one particularly anguished scene, Dempster, 'now fierce with drunken rage', throws his wife out of their house in the middle of the night when she is wearing nothing but her nightgown:

> 'So you think you'll defy me, do you? We'll see how long that will last. Get up madam; out of bed this instant!'
>
> In the close presence of the dreadful man – of this huge crushing force, armed with savage will – poor Janet's desperate defiance all forsook her, and her terrors came back. Trembling she got up, and stood helpless in her night-dress before her husband.
>
> He seized her with his heavy grasp by the shoulder, and pushed her before him.
>
> 'I'll cool your hot spirit for you! I'll teach you to brave me!'
>
> Slowly he pushed her along before him, down-stairs and through the passage, where a small oil-lamp was still flickering. What was he going to do to her? She thought every moment he was going to dash her before him on the ground. But she gave no scream – she only trembled.
>
> He pushed her onto the entrance, and held her firmly in his grasp while he lifted the latch of the door. Then he opened the door a little way, thrust her out, and slammed it behind her.

For a short space, it seemed like a deliverance to Janet. The harsh north-east wind, that blew through her thin night-dress, and sent her long heavy black hair streaming, seemed like the breath of pity after the grasp of that threatening monster. But soon the sense of release from an overpowering terror gave way before the sense of the fate that had really come upon her.

(Chapter Fourteen, *Janet's Repentance*)

The description given to the reader clearly depicts Janet's terror. She is 'seized' and remains 'helpless', and in the dichotomy between the two verbs lies the unfairness of Janet's position. She is vulnerable: a wife with no option but to do as her husband wishes. She supports his tirades against Mr Tryan simply because to do otherwise would be to bring further abuse into her everyday life. She is as much a victim of society's reluctance and inability to help her as she is a victim of her husband's bullying, abusive behaviour. Those who are closest to her seem aware of what she is going through, but remain stagnant and unable to help:

'Mother! Why don't you speak to me?' Janet burst out at last; 'you don't care about my suffering; you are blaming me because I feel – because I am miserable.'

'My child, I am not blaming you – my heart is bleeding for you. Your head is bad this morning – you have had a bad night. Let me make you a cup of tea now. Perhaps you didn't like your breakfast.'

'Yes, that is what you always think, Mother. It is the old story, you think. You don't ask me what it is I have had to bear. You are tired of hearing me. You are cruel, like the rest; everyone is cruel in this world. Nothing but blame – blame, blame; never any pity. God is cruel to have sent me into the world to bear all this misery.'

'Janet, Janet, don't say so. It is not for us to judge; we must submit; we must be thankful for the gift of life.'

(Chapter Fourteen, *Janet's Repentance*)

Even Janet's mother, Mrs Raynor, finds it easier to behave as if her daughter's melancholy stems from an unappetising breakfast, rather than a marriage of brutality. Her belief in her own brand of religious ideology means Mrs Raynor would prefer her daughter to be grateful for the opportunity to live, rather than bemoan the fact that she has to spend her life with a husband who abuses her. Janet's sense of isolation compounds her problems further, and it is only when she has been thrown out and makes the decision not to return to her home, that her mother and the rest of the community are willing to acknowledge the brutal way she has been treated by Mr Dempster. George Eliot tackles Janet's problems by helping her character to seek salvation through morality. Therefore, even while he is dying after an accident caused by his drunken behaviour, Janet tends to her sick husband. She emerges from the role of passive victim to that of active member of her community, and is able to cast aside her submissive stance in order to repent her reliance on alcohol. George Eliot was determined to present the problems of spousal abuse and alcohol addiction in a realistic way, and in doing so she became one of the first writers of her era to tackle such sensitive subjects.

With thoughts of repentance and redemption in mind, I next make my way to Chilvers Coton church. Built of brown stone, parts of the church have their roots in the thirteenth century, but the air raids by the Germans, which destroyed so much of the Midlands in the Second World War, also helped decimate parts of the original building. However, it was later rebuilt with help from German prisoners of war. Chilvers Coton is less than a mile from the centre of Nuneaton, and not only is it the church where George Eliot was baptised, on 29 November 1819, but its grounds are also the place where her parents are buried. Standing beside their grave, I momentarily feel a shudder of gloom blanket me. The green-grey tinge of the stonework seems even colder alongside the bitterness of the early February wind, and even the friendly nod of a passer-by cannot warm me. I head back to the car and with the heater blowing, and the beauty of the church in the shadows to my right, I sit back and consider how important a part religion plays in George Eliot's novels.

Religion

The question of religion was one that engaged George Eliot throughout her lifetime, and so it is perhaps only natural that all of her books should touch upon this theme in some way or another. As a child, she had been brought up to obey the strict moral code of the Bible and her father, in particular, was a great believer in following the words of God. As her education progressed, George Eliot became a devout Evangelical Christian, until her reading of scientific and philosophical books changed her perception of both Christianity and the Bible. She began to believe the Bible was more a historical text to be studied, rather than a moral code to which individuals needed to strictly adhere. Far from being a perfect religion, she began to view Christianity and its dogma as ideology which needed to be challenged. Her refusal to accompany her father to church caused a huge rift in their relationship, and Robert Evans found it difficult to forgive his daughter for her determination to disobey him, and particularly for her insistence on following her own beliefs instead of his.

My own first small act of teenage rebellion came when I declared that I, too, was no longer going to Sunday School. This had far less to do with a philosophical conversion than a realisation that, at 13, I had outgrown the Old Testament colouring books that had once made the soggy biscuits and weak orange squash of break-time bearable. My parents quickly agreed to my request when they realised my equally bored sister and I were the only teenagers left in an ever-dwindling group. But this was the early 1980s, and even in the Welsh valleys the influence of chapel-led Christianity was fading. People were allowed to have more individual beliefs. Families were no longer ripped apart by a difference in ideological and religious thinking. My parents, ever mindful of the value of education and the importance of completing homework on time, were even quicker to agree to my appeal when I pointed out that Sunday afternoons could now be spent completing schoolwork. No such argument existed in the nineteenth century, when Sunday was a day explicitly devoted to religion and prayer. George Eliot was a woman whose beliefs were ahead of her time, and she was more than capable of standing by them and not crumbling in the face of parental disapprobation.

Silas Marner

The difficulties and trials caused by religious differences can be seen most clearly in *Silas Marner*. Published in 1861, the novel's eponymous hero is a dissenter, a Calvinist and weaver living in Lantern Yard.

He arrives in the village of Raveloe following a false accusation of theft. After trusting God to clear his name, Silas does nothing to prove his innocence, but when God does not intervene on his behalf as he is certain he will and Silas is found guilty, he loses his home, his job and his faith. In Raveloe he is seen as an outsider, a man who is at odds with society, an eccentric who turns his back on both the Anglican church and his neighbours. His only passion is the gold he collects from his job as a weaver, hoarding the coins and cherishing them as if they were living beings. He is saved from a life of despair and loneliness, not by religion, but by an abandoned child, Eppie, who wanders into his cottage and falls asleep in front of his fire. Silas begins to take care of the infant as if she is his own. It is Eppie who helps Silas form friendships with the people of Raveloe, and Eppie who gives Silas back his faith. But it is a different faith to the one he had at the beginning of the novel, and it is a faith based on human connections more than a belief in an absolute God who remains impervious to individual circumstances. In Lantern Yard, Silas believed he had been in, 'the altar place of high dispensations'. Later, while living in Raveloe, he looked back upon:

> The white-washed walls; the little pews where well-known figures entered with a subdued rustling, and where first one well-known voice and then another, pitched in a peculiar key of petition, uttered phrases at once occult and familiar, like the amulet worn on the heart; the pulpit where the minister delivered unquestioned doctrine, and swayed to and fro, and handled the book in a long-accustomed manner; the very long pauses between the couplets of the hymn, as it was given out, and the recurrent swell of voices in song: these things had been the channel of divine influences to Marner – they were the fostering home of his religious emotions – they were Christianity and God's kingdom on earth. A weaver who finds hard words in this hymn book knows nothing of abstractions; as the little child knows nothing of parental love, but one knows one face and one lap towards which it stretches its arm for refuge and nurture.
>
> (Chapter Two, *Silas Marner*)

This is very different to the religion that prevails in Raveloe, which is less rigid and an odd mix of superstition and sometimes wavering or sometimes firm belief depending on circumstances:

> The inhabitants of Raveloe were not severely regular in their church-going, and perhaps there was hardly a person in the parish who would not have held that to go to church every Sunday in the calendar would have shown a greedy desire to stand well with Heaven, and get an undue advantage over their neighbours – a wish to be better than the 'common run', that would have implied a reflection on those who had had godfathers and godmothers as well as themselves, and had an equal right to the burying-service. At the same time, it was understood to be requisite for all who were not household servants, or young men, to take the sacrament at one of the great festivals: Squire Cass himself took it on Christmas-day; while those who were held to be 'good livers' went to church with greater, though still with moderate, frequency. Mrs Winthrop was one of these; she was in all respects a woman of scrupulous conscience, so eager for duties that life seemed to offer them too scantily unless she rose at half-past four, though this threw a scarcity of work over the more advanced hours of the morning, which it was a constant problem with her to remove.
>
> (Chapter Ten, *Silas Marner*)

It is Dolly Winthrop who gently persuades Silas to once again have contact with the outside world. She guides him in his parenting of Eppie, and encourages him to take his adopted daughter to church so that she may be christened. This is Silas's first introduction to the religion of Raveloe, and it serves as a means of creating links between Silas and the community he had hitherto hidden from. In this way, the church and the religion upon which it depends does not so much enlighten Silas as to the word of God, but instead serves to let him once more enjoy the touch of human kindness and kinship.

Belief in God

After completing *Silas Marner*, readers are very much left with the feeling that George Eliot has not wished to provide an answer to the question concerning the existence of God. Indeed, by the end of the novel, we are essentially no wiser as to the writer's own thoughts on this topic than we were at the beginning. Instead, George Eliot has cleverly posed *the reader* several important questions. She asks them to look beyond the existence of God and their thoughts on this issue, and to consider instead the nature of their own relationship with religion and to ruminate on the fact that life can exist without an omnipotent God who can be blamed for all of life's troubles. Silas leaves Lantern Yard blaming God for not rescuing him from the situation he finds himself in. Yet ultimately, after many years of isolation, Silas is saved from misery through human contact with Dolly Winthrop and Eppie. Perhaps one of the most important messages George Eliot leaves her readers to contemplate after reading *Silas Marner* is that regardless of the church they might worship in, or the prayers they might utter, it is their interaction with others that is of the greatest importance.

Arbury Hall

After feeling suitably warmed by the running of the car engine, and with my head still full of religion, I decide to pay a visit to Arbury Hall, the workplace of George Eliot's father, Robert Evans. The many pictures I have seen of the hall reveal it to be a majestically Gothic-looking building. Even the stable doorway was based on a design by Sir Christopher Wren. I am disappointed, therefore, to find upon my arrival at Arbury that it is closed for the season. Two lone winter workers, their grey silhouettes shawled in opaque white, head towards the horizon and towards the entrance of Arbury, but today I will not be able to follow in their footsteps. The only glimpse I am allowed is of the Gothic-styled arch at the top of the visitors' drive. It gives a tantalising hint of the architectural drama that is, for today at least, denied to me.

In spite of my disappointment, I am eager to visit Astley, a small village a few minutes' drive away. The journey there takes me along small winding roads, past bare, black hedgerows and banks of murky green. For the first time I feel nearer to the shadow of George Eliot than ever before and I am able to imagine her walking along roadsides roughened by cartwheels, or sitting beside her father as he surveyed the land of his employers, the Newdigate family. It is a feeling which increases as I pull up alongside St Mary the Virgin church, the place where George Eliot's parents were married. From where I am parked, the church tower is just visible over the top of a wall dressed in skirts of soft green ivy. But as I walk nearer to the church, the path that leads me to its main door branches outwards, until the building is visible in all its grey stone beauty.

It is easy to imagine the inside of this building adding solemnity and sobriety to any religious service. Strips of light and shade fall across the aisle, marking the way daylight turns to darkness and the passage of time as the months turn to years.

Mr Gilfil's Love-Story

It is not just the church but Astley itself that is important to readers of George Eliot, particularly because the village became her inspiration for Knebley in *Mr Gilfil's Love-Story* in *Scenes of Clerical Life*. Mr Gilfil is the vicar for both the villages of Knebley and Shepperton, and it becomes effortless for the reader to picture him from the writer's humorously direct description of her creation:

> You already suspect that the Vicar did not shine in the more spiritual functions of his office; and indeed; the utmost I can say for him in this respect is, that he performed those functions with undeviating attention to brevity and despatch. He had a large heap of short sermons, rather yellow and worn at the edges from which he took two every Sunday, securing perfect impartiality in the selection by taking them as they came, without reference to topics; and having preached one of these sermons at Shepperton in the morning, he mounted his horse and rode hastily with the other in his pocket to Knebley, where he officiated in a wonderful little church, with a checkered pavement which had once rung to the iron tread of military monks, with coats of arms in clusters on the lofty roof, marble warriors and their wives without noses occupying a large proportion of the area, and the twelve apostles with their heads very much on one side, holding didactic ribbons, painted in fresco on the walls. Here, in an absence of mind to which

he was prone, Mr Gilfil would sometimes forget to take off his spurs before putting on his surplice, and only become aware of the omission by feeling something mysteriously tugging at the skirts of that garment as he stepped into that reading-desk. But the Knebley farmers would as soon have thought of criticising the moon as their pastor. He belonged to the course of nature, like markets and toll-gates and dirty bank-notes; and being a vicar his claim on their veneration had never been counteracted by an exasperating claim on their pockets.

(Chapter One, *Mr Gilfil's Love-Story*)

Mr Gilfil is not an exacting vicar and does not appear to demand a great deal from his parishioners. In return, the churchgoers of Knebley turn a blind eye to their vicar's frequent lapses in etiquette, especially when he forgets to remove his spurs before preaching to them, and they also forgive him for the brevity and repetitive nature of his sermons. They believe him to be as natural a part of life as 'toll-gates and dirty bank-notes', and therefore it never seems to enter their heads to challenge him as to his many little foibles. The members of his congregation favour him in particular because he does not make a call upon their pockets and purses for money, and in this way Gilfil almost guarantees himself the trust and following of the people of Knebley. George Eliot's careful and clever piece of description allows the reader an insight into the lives and minds of the villagers.

Griff House

It would have been impossible to leave the area of Nuneaton without first calling at George Eliot's childhood home, Griff House. It came as something of a disappointment when I first discovered it had long been masquerading as a Beefeater Grill Steak Restaurant. My first thought was to wonder if George Eliot had ever even liked beef enough for her once-beloved home to now be dedicated to the eating of it. With no real way of finding out the answer to such a question, I decide to visit anyway, in the hope of at least satisfying myself that the restaurant has kept some small nod to its heritage on display.

The blur and whirr of the weekend traffic, which stops and starts along the road outside, makes me worry I will find it impossible to imagine the writer and her family living and working in their house. My one consolation comes from the fact that even at a distance, it is obvious that in overall shape at least, Griff House can be easily identified. The pointed roof still stands to the left, and sash windows still decorate the front of the building. The inside of the pub essentially belongs to the twenty-first century, with Wi-Fi and music that can do nothing to bring back the shadow of nineteenth-century life. My hopes lie instead in the grounds of the pub, and the land on which the Evans children must once have played. I feel even more satisfied when I read that the pub chain has donated a substantial amount to the George Eliot Fellowship fund in order to raise money for the building of a heritage centre behind the restaurant. On rough, stony land, separated only by a stone wall from the pub, some outbuildings once used by Robert Evans lie untouched. It is hoped that these can eventually be turned into a memorial dedicated to all things related to the writer. In this accomplishment at least, it will feel as if George Eliot's childhood home has been partly restored to her, particularly since her love of the area in which she grew up is surely powerful enough to transcend both time and historical differences.

As I make my way back to Swansea, George Eliot's understanding of the importance of childhood memories sends me on a detour to the South Wales valleys, the town of Brynmawr and my own childhood home. It is almost five years since I have been back to the house where I grew up, and although when I arrive, the faint strands of left-over winter sun are dimming to dusk, I can still see enough of my old home to trace the differences. For some reason I become unreasonably overwrought at the fact that the wooden sign which had the numbers 153 etched upon it has been removed, to be replaced with a slate one bearing the words 'laughter' and 'love'. These are sentiments I am usually in favour of, yet incongruously, they appear traitorous and tainted with betrayal. I wonder how I would feel if, like George Eliot, I came back to discover my house was now a restaurant and pub.

When my parents first bought the terrace on Worcester Street, my mum insisted that my dad paint it pink and from then on, she gloried in the fact that it was the only building in the entire town to be painted such a shade. I loved the rich potency of its striking colour, but my tomboy twin sister often winced at having to admit to living in a house whose hue matched that of a rose. I sensed that colour had the power to brighten days that could be tarnished by small-town discord and relished in the uniqueness of living in the town's first truly colourful house. The 1960s had only just been discarded, and although colour had begun to flourish with an abundance in valley fashion, the long rows of terraces that perched like anxious crows on slanting wires were a mottled blend of grey and brown. Our house was a flicker of colour in an otherwise murky, muddy sea.

If George Eliot enjoyed escaping to the attic, I enjoyed escaping to my bedroom. Like a silent shadow I revelled in the solitude of my own company. Watching, waiting and listening enabled me to learn the secrets of the adult world. Home was where I felt safe and comfortable, which is why the home I lived in from birth until I was 23 remains so important to me, even all these years later. It is why I understand so well George Eliot's beliefs in the importance of home, which can be traced throughout her novels:

> A human life, I think, should be well rooted in some spot of a native land, where it may get the love of tender kinship for the face of the earth, for the labours men go forth to, for the sounds and accents that haunt it, for whatever will give that early home a familiar unmistakable difference amidst the future widening of knowledge: a spot where the definiteness of early memories may be inwrought with affection, and kindly acquaintance with all neighbours, even to the dogs and donkeys, may spread not by sentimental effort and reflection, but as a sweet habit of the blood. At five years old, mortals are not prepared to be citizens of the world, to be stimulated by abstract nouns, to soar above preference into impartiality; and that prejudice in favour of milk with which we blindly begin, is a type of the way body and soul must get nourished at least for a time. The best introduction to astronomy is to think of the nightly heavens as a little lot of stars belonging to one's own homestead.
>
> (Part One, Chapter Three, *Daniel Deronda*)

Chapter Three

In which George Eliot's importance as a writer, an academic, and a social and political thinker is considered

*...and it is a narrow mind which cannot look at a subject
from various points of view*

(*Middlemarch*)

George Eliot's later years in London, spent, in part, entertaining academics and scholars at her home, the Priory, in the suburb of St John's Wood, were in many ways a contradiction of her birth in rural Warwickshire. In London, Eliot's Sundays were dedicated to debate and rigorous discussion with some of the leading politicians and thinkers of nineteenth-century Britain. Figures such as Liberal Party leader William Gladstone, and the writer Leslie Stephen, father of the future Virginia Woolf, who would herself prove to be a formidable intellectual opponent, all impatiently waited their turn to vocally spar with a woman who had once been shunned by society for her less-than-conventional marriage arrangements. Yet now these great thinkers gathered with alacrity, eager to challenge George Eliot, to question her and to parley. Most important of all, they wanted to experience for themselves the opportunity to exchange views with a woman as forthright and as confident as she was at a time when many women struggled to be heard above the roar of the male voice.

The role of women

For many, George Eliot was something of an anomaly. As a woman she was so unlike many others of her gender, who were forced to abide by the nineteenth-century rules that kept women quietly by the hearth and ensured only men enjoyed a wider political, economic and social circle. It was a topic that was debated widely in the literature of the day, with poets such as Coventry Patmore, Alfred Tennyson, and Elizabeth Barrett Browning, all using their poetry as a means of exploring the 'woman question'. Similarly, novelists such as Charlotte and Anne Brontë, Thomas Hardy and George Eliot believed their texts could help draw attention to the frustrations women faced when they were marginalised because of their gender, or forced to repress the very parts of their personalities that made them unique.

Coventry Patmore

Coventry Patmore's contribution to the debate was not only in agreeing with the generally held belief that middle-class women served society best when they remained obedient and subservient 'angels', but in also helping to perpetuate the ideal of the perfect woman. Patmore felt true wives should behave as heavenly beings, paragons who blessed upstanding households with their calm and patient nature and who helped to make the lives of their husbands and sons easier by restoring familial tranquillity. In turn, it was believed this would allow their spouses the time they needed to recover from a demanding career in the wider world of work, ensuring therefore that upon their return home, they would be free to unwind, safe in the knowledge that their wives were taking care of all other household concerns. However, according to Patmore, women needed to do more than just this. They also needed to be visions of beauty, whose behaviour was modelled on nothing less than an angelic and saintly creature who betrayed no moral faults. In his poem *The Angel in the House* (1854), Patmore wrote,

> But when I look on her and hope
> To tell with joy what I admire,
> My thoughts lie cramp'd in narrow scope,
> Or in the feeble birth expire;
> No mystery of well-woven speech,
> No simplest phrase of tenderest fall,
> No liken'd excellence can reach
> Her, thee most excellent of all,
> The best half of creation's best,

Its heart to feel, its eye to see,
The crown and complex of the rest,
Its aim and its epitome.
Nay, might I utter my conceit,
'Twere after all a vulgar song,
For she's so simply, subtly sweet,
My deepest rapture does her wrong.
Yet it is now my chosen task
To sing her worth as Maid and Wife;
Nor happier post than this I ask.
To live a laureate all my life.

Patmore's focus on words and phrases such as 'simply, subtly sweet', and his desire to sing of his wife's worth as a 'Maid', all highlight his need to see women as having been transfixed in a prepubescent state. These women, who were expected to run busy households, keep a firm grip on the family budget and soothe the furrowed brow of their put-upon husbands, had to paradoxically produce a litter of children all whilst remaining perplexingly simple, devoid of knowledge, and in a state of constant innocence.

Aurora Leigh

Refreshingly, Elizabeth Barrett Browning used her poem *Aurora Leigh*, written in 1856, as a means by which she could comment on the narrow domestic sphere many men in the nineteenth century expected women to inhabit. She highlighted the fact that females were meant to do so without complaint. Compliancy was, after all, expected to be a natural part of a female's inner being. In her poem, Barrett Browning spent time exploring the various attributes women were expected to have, or at the very least the supposed 'natural' qualities that many men took for granted:

Women know
The way to rear up children (to be just),
They know a simple, merry, tender knack
Of tying sashes, fitting baby-shoes,
And string pretty words that make no sense,

And kissing full sense into empty words,
Which things are corals to cut life upon,
Although such trifles: children learn by such,
Love's holy earnest in a pretty play
And get not over-early solemnised,
But seeing, as in a rose-bush, Love's Divine
Which burns and hurts not, - a single bloom, -
Become aware and unafraid of Love,
Such good do mothers.
>   (First Book, Lines 47-60, *Aurora Leigh*)

Here, the reader senses that although Barrett Browning understood the natural instincts of a mother, unlike Coventry Patmore she never once believed that a woman's role as a care-giver was all she had to offer. Instead, not only was Barrett Browning willing to elevate the importance of a mother's role to more than mere nurturer, ('Children learn by such'), but she was also aware of the frustrations women faced when they yearned for a life for themselves outside of the nursery and home. She subverted the natural assumption made by many nineteenth-century males that women were inherently foolish, by drawing attention to the undeniable words of wisdom that mothers were capable of passing on to their children.

When Aurora is left orphaned following the death of her father, she is forced to leave the beauty of her life, 'Among the mountains above Pelago', in order to move to England,

Then, land! – then England! Oh, the frosty cliffs
Looked cold upon me, could I find a home
Among those mean red houses through the fog?
>   (First Book, Lines 251-253, *Aurora Leigh*)

She is forced to take up residence with her aunt, who as Aurora is astute enough to point out,

…had lived, we'll say,
A harmless life, she called a virtuous life,
A quiet life, which was not life at all,
(but that she had not lived enough to know)
>   (First Book, Lines 287-290, *Aurora Leigh*)

Aurora is questioning not only her aunt's lack of life experience, but also that of anyone claiming to live by a particular set of rules, when in reality they have not experienced any other type of life with which they can accurately compare them. The restrictions placed upon Aurora irritate her, forced as she is to live by her aunt's narrow-minded beliefs and strict adherence to conformity, especially concerning the education of young girls on the cusp of womanhood:

> and I drew…costumes
> From French engravings, nereids neatly draped,
> …I washed in …
> Landscapes from nature …
> I danced the polka and Cellarius,
> Spun glass, stuffed birds, and modelled flowers in wax,
> Because she liked accomplishments in girls.
> I read a score of books on womanhood
> To prove if women do not think at all,
> They may teach thinking, (to a maiden-aunt
> Or else the author) – books that boldly assert
> Their right of comprehending husband's talk
> When not too deep, and even of answering
> With pretty 'may it please you,' or 'so it is,' –
> Their rapid insight and fine aptitude
> Particular worth and general missionariness,
> As long as they keep quiet by the fire
> And never say 'no' when the world says 'aye,'
> For that is fatal,
>
> (First Book, Lines 420-438, *Aurora Leigh*)

The insightfulness shown here by Aurora would have provided the contemporary reader with an informed understanding of Elizabeth Barrett Browning's own views on the education of young women, and on the benefits of allowing them to contribute to healthy political and social debate. Many women would have applauded such views. Unfortunately, however, Barrett Browning was in the minority in her belief that the right of a woman to express her views was of paramount importance. The majority of a patriarchal-led nineteenth-century society believed that as long as the daily lives of women were filled with useful but petty tasks, as long as they challenged no-one and agreed with the beliefs of the dominant male in their life, and as long as they knew their place was to sit quietly by the fireside, it might be deemed appropriate for them to only occasionally voice their opinion.

When she discovers her father's library of books, which have been stored at her aunt's home, Aurora escapes into an inner world that affords her the independence and freedom she longs for. Through reading about the ideas and beliefs which provide a stepping stone towards the freedom she craves, Aurora is allowed to discover her life's worth, and therefore adds value to her daily existence without the aid of a male:

> Books, books, books!
> I had found the secret of a garret-room
> Piled high with cases in my father's name,
> Piled high, packed large, – where, creeping in and out,
> Among the giant fossils of my past,
> Like some small nimble mouse between the ribs
> Of a mastadon, I nibbled here and there
> At this or that box, pulling through the gap,
> In heats of terror, haste, victorious joy,
> The first book first...
> My books! At last because the time was ripe,
> I chanced upon the poets.
>> (First Book, Lines 833-844, *Aurora Leigh*)

Through her own endeavours and determination, Aurora is later rewarded and given the opportunity to live the life she has chosen, away from the confines of male-imposed domesticity. By the opening of the Third Book, three years have passed and the protagonist has found herself some rooms in Kensington, from where she supports herself as a freelance writer. Barrett Browning's text exposes Aurora's maturity – her ability to criticise her own faults, to be self-aware and short on foolishness are pleasingly obvious:

> I worked with patience, which means almost power:
> I did some excellent things indifferently,
> Some bad things excellently. Both were praised,
> The latter loudest.
>> (Third Book, Lines 204-207, *Aurora Leigh*)

Before becoming a full-time novelist, George Eliot herself was an editor and contributor to reviews and journals. In January 1857 she contributed a review of *Aurora Leigh* to the *Westminster Review,* and in spite of certain misgivings mainly regarding the literary trope of male blindness as used by Charlotte Brontë in *Jane Eyre,* Eliot's review was a favourable one. Although she commented that:

> The story of Aurora Leigh has no other merits than that of offering certain elements of life and certain situations which are peculiarly fitted to call forth the writer's rich thought and experience...

Her overwhelming response was one of praise and delight at the 'rich melodious song of the rare poem'. She concluded her review with a note of deep satisfaction:

> The most striking characteristic of 'Aurora Leigh', distinguishing it from the larger proportion of that contemporary poetry which wins the applause of reviewers, is, that its melody, fancy, and imagination – what we may call its poetical body – is everywhere informed by a soul, namely, by genuine thought and feeling. There is no petty striving after special effects, no heaping up of images for their own sake, no trivial pay of fancy run quite astray from the control of deeper sensibility; there is simply a full mind pouring itself out in song as is its natural and easiest medium. The mind has far-stretching thoughts, its abundant treasure of well-digested learning, its acute observation of life, its yearning sympathy with multi-form human sorrow, its state of personal domestic love and joy; and these are given out in a delightful alternation of pathos, reflection, satire playful or pungent and picturesque description, which carries us with swifter pulses than usual through four hundred pages, and makes us sorry to find ourselves in the end...it has the calm, even flow of a broad river, not the spray and rainbow of a mountain torrent.

George Eliot's acknowledgement of Barrett Browning's 'thought and feeling', combined with her 'deep-digested' learning, are as much an insight into her own preoccupations as they are of the poet's. George Eliot never failed to be impressed with women who were able to display their intellectual and academic merits through a creative medium, and those who had the confidence to share their work remained of particular importance.

The Princess

Alfred Tennyson's contemplation on women and the role they should be accorded in the nineteenth century can be most clearly seen in his poem *The Princess*. Published in 1847, it is a narrative poem, which in spite of the serious nature of the social questions posed within its lines, is partly comic in nature. It tells the story of a princess, who upon deciding to rid herself forever of the company of men, founds a female-only university and swears she will dedicate the rest of her life to the education of women with similar beliefs. However, in spite of all her protestations, the princess ends the poem by marrying the prince to whom she was previously betrothed. This led some contemporary readers to criticise Tennyson for his apparently less-than-sympathetic view of those women who yearned for something more than marriage and motherhood. Those readers who were fighting for change felt that the ending mocked their beliefs, with its suggestion that for all their protestations, a woman's ultimate happiness came from the very thing they pretended to despise – the opportunity to be married, and the renouncing of all other aspects of themselves in order to run a household of their own.

In Part Five of the poem, women are compared to prey, hunted in packs for their beauty:

> Look you, Sir!
> Man is the hunter; woman is his game;
> The sleek and shining creatures of the chase.
> We hunt them for the beauty of their skins;
> They love us for it, and we ride them down.

Although these lines are spoken by the king, there is still something very disquieting about a mouthpiece which is used to talk of 'hunting' down women, and it was exactly this sentiment which made some contemporary readers feel uncomfortable. In Part Five, the king continues with his diatribe about the role of women when he adds:

> Man for the field and woman for the hearth:
> Man for the sword and for the needle she:
> Man with the head and woman with the heart:
> Man to command and woman to obey;
> All else confusion.

Several lines later, the king completes his summing up on the differences between the genders by concluding:

> Besides, the woman wed is not as we,
> But suffers change of frame. A lusty brace
> Of twins may weed her of her folly. Boy,
> The bearing and training of a child
> Is woman's wisdom.

According to the king, a woman's folly was her apparent determination to seek independence away from that which should be her true calling: obtaining a husband and a home. In response to his critics, Tennyson claimed that the king's ideas did not reflect his own views on the role of women in society. However, many readers remained unconvinced, leading the poet to add further additions, such as the songs sung by the women, which reaffirmed their practical natures and intelligence. If Tennyson believed his views regarding female independence were made obvious in the poem, he was mistaken and readers have continued to criticise him for his apparently anti-feminist views.

Charlotte Brontë

In contrast, Charlotte Brontë's eponymous protagonist Jane Eyre and George Eliot's Maggie Tulliver each provide their creators with the ideal means by which to discuss further the need for gender equality. As a result, the reader is left in no doubt as to which side of the argument Brontë and George Eliot came down upon when the idea of female equality and women's rights to an education were being questioned.

Chapter Three

In *Jane Eyre* (1847), Jane's restless nature, her desire for freedom and her disappointment at the lack of independence offered to women, particularly those who found themselves working as a governess, are all emphasised by her relentless pacing around the corridors and grounds of Thornfield Hall. In Chapter Twelve of Volume One, she ponders:

> Who blames me? Many, no doubt: and I shall be called discontented. I could not help it; the restlessness was in my nature; it agitated me to pain sometimes. Then my sole relief was to walk along the corridor of the third story, backwards and forwards, safe in the silence and solitude of the spot, and allow my mind's eye to dwell on whatever bright visions rose before it...
>
> It is in vain to say human beings ought to be satisfied with tranquillity: they must have action; and they will make it if they cannot find it. Millions are condemned to a stiller doom than mine, and millions are in silent revolt against their lot. Nobody knows how many rebellions beside political rebellions ferment in the masses of life which people earth. Women are supposed to be very calm generally: but women feel just as men feel; they need exercise for their faculties, and a field for their efforts as much as their brothers do; they suffer from too rigid a restraint, too absolute a stagnation, precisely as men would suffer; and it is narrow-minded in their more privileged fellow-creatures to say that they ought to confine themselves to making puddings and knitting stockings, to playing on the piano and embroidering bags. It is thoughtless to condemn them, or laugh at them, if they seek to do more or learn more than custom has pronounced necessary for their sex.

This is a gloriously compassionate call to arms, and one in which Brontë merges her own view of womanhood with that of her creation. Both Jane Eyre and Charlotte Brontë believed that women's sanity, indeed their very survival, depended on their ability to be educated, to be trusted and to be accorded more freedom than they were usually allowed in households ruled by men.

Maggie Tulliver

Published thirteen years later than *Jane Eyre* in 1860, George Eliot's second novel and third publication, *The Mill on the Floss*, has at its heart a protagonist equally as restless as Jane Eyre. When she is a young girl, Maggie finds it difficult to do as she is asked, a fact that is reflected by her unruly hair, which, as her mother Mrs Tulliver laments in Chapter Two:

> won't curl all I can do with it, and she's so franzy about having it put i' paper, and I've such work as niver was to make her stand and have it pinched with th' irons.

Maggie's restlessness, and her inability to listen to her mother's seemingly endless and trivial instructions, derive partly from her wish to be educated. It is a desire made worse by the fact that it is her brother Tom who is to receive an education, in spite of being what his own father describes as 'a bit slowish', and not having 'the right sort o' brains for a smart fellow'. Society has decreed, however, that regardless of a girl's intelligence and in spite of the lack of intellect accorded to a young boy, it is always the male who should be schooled in Humanities, Mathematics and the Sciences. A girl must be mindful to put away her bonnet carefully and try to flatten the unruly kinks and curls in her hair – none of which Maggie manages – and leave the academic world of debate, great literature and philosophy to the opposite sex. Maggie's frustrations derive from her inquisitive nature and her natural thirst for knowledge. Therefore, when Mr Riley, the auctioneer, arrives to give Mr and Mrs Tulliver advice regarding Tom's education, Maggie is keen to impress him. In Chapter Three she begins to 'flush with triumphant excitement', when she hears her father speak well of her to Mr Riley, especially when he concludes:

> 'She understands what one's talking about so as never was. And you should hear her read – straight off, as if she knowed it all beforehand. An' allays at her book! But it's bad – it's bad,' Mr Tulliver added sadly, checking this blameable exultation; 'a woman's no business wi' being so clever; it'll turn to trouble, I doubt. But, bless you!' – here this humble exultation was clearly recovering the mastery – 'she'll read

the books and understand 'em, better nor half the folks as
are growed up.'

In spite of her father's belief that an educated female can only lead to
badness, Maggie bristles in delight when hearing her father praise her
intellectual ability. Keen to take advantage of the moment and prove her
worth to Mr Riley, she soon regales him with her own interpretation of
the illustrations in the book she has been reading:

> 'Oh, I'll tell you what that means. It's a dreadful picture
> isn't it? But I can't help looking at it. That old woman in
> the water's a witch – they've put her in to find out whether
> she's a witch or no, and if she swims she's a witch, and if
> she's drowned – and killed, you know – she's innocent, and
> not a witch, but only a poor silly old woman. But what good
> would it do her then, you know, when she drowned?'

Far from being impressed at such a succinct summing up, or to even
feel it remarkable that a young girl like Maggie Tulliver could so easily
access Daniel Defoe's *The History Of The Devil*, Mr Riley irks the
young girl who wants nothing more from him than his approbation or a
compliment, by belittling her:

> 'Well,' said Mr. Riley in an admonitory, patronising tone,
> as he patted Maggie on the head, 'I advise you to put by the
> "History of the Devil," and read some prettier book. Have
> you no prettier books?'

After some discussion and thought, Mr Riley concludes that the *Pilgrim's
Progress* would be much more suitable as a text for Maggie, but not
before she alarms and, indeed, goes so far as to contradict him, with her
insistence that there is much to discover about the Devil even in John
Bunyon's novel.

George Eliot was apparently determined to pit male against female
in her ongoing campaign to promote every woman's right to receive an
education as thorough as that of a man. And even when they were not yet
fully matured, she was not afraid to show that her female protagonists
had the intelligence and tenacity to prove that those males who quibbled

and patronised them could be proved wrong in the argument for denying a woman the right to freedom and equality.

George Eliot cared little for the etiquette that forced itself with such habitual rigour upon many women trying to forge a life for themselves in nineteenth-century Britain – women who were harnessed not just by the strict codes of a patriarchal society, but also by the very clothes their bodies were physically limited by. The corsets and petticoats that shackled their bodies were a reflection of the rules of a society that undoubtedly favoured offering its right to freedom to men only.

Social concerns

As a writer, George Eliot was determined to use her skills for more than mere entertainment. Her goal was to enhance her readers' understanding of the social concerns that impacted upon the lives of those individuals who lacked the ability or opportunity to speak for themselves. Her legacy remains not just in the novels she left behind, but also in the vast body of correspondence and literary reviews that bear her name, alongside the rigorous conversations for which she was renowned. Perhaps one of the most interesting questions to pose is how did George Eliot, born into relative obscurity and with little in her family history to suggest otherwise, become one of the most highly-regarded writers and thinkers of the nineteenth century?

Chapter Four

In which George Eliot is born and thrives, and her childhood surroundings leave an indelible mark on her conscience

I cherish my childish loves, the memory of that warm little nest where my affections were fledged.
(*Impressions of Theophrastus Such*)

When Mary Ann Evans was born on 22 November 1819 in rural Warwickshire, there was little about her birth to suggest her life would be as full of controversy and incident as it was. She was born in a small farmhouse to Robert Evans and his second wife Christiana (née Pearson), his first wife Harriet (née Poynton) having died in 1809. The farmhouse was stone-built, made to resist the seasons, and although not large, was comfortable and considered a suitable abode for the land agent of the Newdigate family of Arbury Hall, upon whose estate the cottage was situated.

The Newdigate family and the Gothic

Arbury Hall had belonged to the Newdigate family since the sixteenth century and at the time of Robert Evans' employment, it appeared very much as it does today: an imposing mansion, Elizabethan in origin, with additional features commissioned by Sir Roger Newdigate and inspired by the Gothic revival of the late eighteenth century.

The revival of Gothic architecture began as early as the 1740s in Great Britain and lasted until the latter part of the nineteenth century. It became popular for those homeowners who could afford it to add fan vaults,

35

finials and ornate mouldings to their properties. Some landowners went so far as to build 'ancient' monastic ruins in their grounds, or tormented visitors with stories of wailing spectres and headless monks they had supposedly seen floating through the dark night sky. Such architectural features went hand in hand with a revival of Gothic poetry, and poets such as John Keats were able to exploit their readers' fascination for literature concerned with morbidity, sorrow and death. In his narrative poem *Isabella*, or *The Pot of Basil*, written in 1818, Keats tells the tale of a young woman intended for marriage to a rich nobleman. However, she falls in love with Lorenzo, a servant. When her brothers discover the truth about their sister's feelings they are incensed, and in a fit of rage, murder Lorenzo and secretly bury his body. In a literary trope familiar to readers of Gothic fiction, Lorenzo's ghost then appears to Isabella, in order to reveal the truth. She exhumes his body, takes his head, and buries it beneath a basil plant, which she tends obsessively whilst pining for her loved one:

> Then in a silken scarf, - sweet with the dews
> Of precious flowers pluck'd in Araby,
> And divine liquids come with odorous ooze
> Through the cold serpent pipe refreshfully, -
> She wrapp'd it up; and for its tomb did choose
> A garden-pot, wherein she laid it by,
> And cover'd it with mould, and o'er it set
> Sweet Basil, which her tears kept ever wet.
> (Verse 52, Lines 409-416, *Isabella* or *The Pot of Basil*)

Arbury Hall remained an inspiration to George Eliot long after she had moved away from the area, and its Gothic influence can perhaps be seen most clearly in *Scenes of Clerical Life* and in her description of Cheveral Manor, whose 'great gothic windows' reflect those that she would have remembered from Arbury Hall. Of Cheveral Manor, she wrote:

> And a charming picture Cheveral Manor would have made
> that evening if an English Watteau had been there to paint
> it; the castellated house of grey tinted stone, with the
> flickering sunbeams sending dashes of golden light across

the many-shaped panes in the mullioned windows, and a great beech leaning athwart one of the flanking towers, and breaking with its dark flattened boughs, the too formal symmetry of the front; the broad gravel walk winding on the right, by a row of tall pines, alongside the pool – on the left branching out among swelling grassing mounds, surmounted by clumps of trees, where the red trunk of the scotch fir glows in the sunlight against the bright green of limes and acacias; the great pool, where a pair of swans are swimming lazily with one leg tucked under a wing...

Seen from the great Gothic windows of the dining-room, they had much more definiteness of outline, and were distinctly visible to the three gentlemen sipping their claret there, as two fair women in whom all three had a personal interest. These gentlemen were a group worth considering attentively; but anyone entering that dining-room for the first time, would perhaps have had his attention even more strongly arrested by the room itself, which was so bare of furniture that it impressed one with its architectural beauty like a cathedral. A piece of matting stretched from door to door, a bit of worn carpet under the dining-table, and a side-board in a deep recess, did not detain the eye for a moment from the lofty groined ceiling, with its richly-carved pendants, all of creamy white, relieved here and there by touches of gold. On one side, this lofty ceiling was supported by pillars and arches, beyond which a lower ceiling, a miniature copy of the higher one, covered the square projection which, with its three large pointed windows, formed the central feature of the building. The room looked less a place to dine in than a piece of space enclosed simply for the sake of a beautiful outline; and the small dining-table, with the party round it, seemed an odd and insignificant accident, rather than anything connected with the original purpose of the apartment.

(Chapter Two, *Mr Gilfil's Love-Story*)

No doubt George Eliot's memories, alongside her powerful ability to capture the imagination of her reader, both play a part in the beauty of her vivid portrayal of Cheveral Manor in this passage. However, what it is much easier to assume with certainty is that by 1820, and with his family growing both in number and size – between his two marriages, George Eliot was her father's fifth child and third daughter – a house move was deemed necessary by the Evans family.

A family move

When she was only four months old, George Eliot's family moved to Griff House in south Nuneaton. It was to be her home for the next twenty-one years, and from this Georgian house some of the writer's most important memories were formed. The house was well-endowed with bedrooms – there were eight in total, and in the summer months the substantial garden bloomed with colour. Although its size and style – the house was relatively large and built not of stone but of red brick – might in some ways have suggested that Robert Evans' social circumstances were on the up, the cluster of outbuildings and farming paraphernalia that jostled for space in the land immediately surrounding the house revealed the truth – that as a privileged member of the Newdigate family's estate team, Robert Evans had reached the pinnacle of his career. His employer, Francis Parker-Newdigate trusted Robert Evans implicitly, and recognised him for the trustworthy, shrewd and hard-working man of the land that he was. More importantly, perhaps, is the fact that Griff House became a reflection not just of the Evans family's station in life, and of Robert Evans' role as a successful and well-respected land agent, but also an indication as to the social and economic situation that existed in much of the Midlands at the beginning of the nineteenth century.

There is a tendency to picture the land around Nuneaton at the time of the Evans family's move to Griff House as a rustic, somewhat bucolic place, and to visualise the people who lived there as spending a halcyon existence, thriving either as farmers, labourers, or making a living through running a cottage industry. This was, after all, a time when Great Britain was on the very cusp of the Industrial Revolution, and the impact of mechanised manufacturing had yet to be felt outside of the cities and larger towns. We know that George Eliot often accompanied her father on his horse and cart as he travelled to

Arbury Hall and surveyed the land over which he had authority, and it is tempting, therefore, to imagine the writer as a young girl, being driven through swathes of arable land, or fields full of herds of cattle and sheep put to pasture, surveying the countryside that would later influence her writing.

Perhaps this is seen most particularly in her description of Raveloe, the village near the stone cottage of the weaver, Silas Marner, who at the turn of the nineteenth century, 'In the days when the spinning-wheels hummed busily in the farmhouses' still made a living through weaving by hand:

> And Raveloe was a village where many of the old echoes lingered, undrowned by new voices. Not that it was one of those barren parishes lying on the outskirts of civilization – inhabited by meagre sheep and thinly-scattered shepherds; on the contrary, it lay in the rich central plain of what we are pleased to call Merry England, and held farms which, speaking from a spiritual point of view, paid highly desirable tithes. But it was nestled in a snug well-wooded hollow, quite an hour's journey on horseback from any turnpike, where it was never reached by the vibrations of the coach-horn, or of public opinion. It was an important looking village, with a fine old church and large churchyard in the heart of it, and two or three large brick and stone homesteads, with well-walled orchards and ornamental weather-cocks, standing close upon the road, and lifting more imposing fronts than the rectory, which peeped from among the trees on the other side of the churchyard: – a village which showed at once the summits of its social life.
>
> (Chapter One, *Silas Marner*)

But in contrast to Raveloe's isolated position, 'an hour's journey on horseback from any turnpike', Arbury Hall and its surroundings were already displaying the typical signs of industrialisation. The land belonging to the Newdigate family was nothing if not rich in coal mining opportunities, and the nearby canal – a favourite place of play for George Eliot and her cherished elder brother Isaac when he deigned to spend time with his sister – was an ideal water source. Built by Sir Roger

Newdigate, the Griff Canal enabled coal taken from the seams of the land surrounding Arbury Hall to be transported around the rest of the country. As well as playing an important part in the economy of the Arbury Estate, its workers, and the Newdigate family, the Griff Canal was also a source of inspiration for George Eliot, who wrote about it in her sonnet sequence, *Brother and Sister:*

> Our brown canal was endless to my thought;
> And on its banks I sat in dreamy peace,
> Unknowing how the good I loved was wrought,
> Untroubled by the fear that it would cease.
>
> Slowly the barges floated into view
> Rounding a grassy hill to me sublime
> With some Unknown beyond it, whither flew
> The parting cuckoo toward a fresh spring time.
>
> The wide-arched bridge, the scented elder flowers,
> The wondrous watery rings that died too soon,
> The echoes of the quarry, the still hours
> With white robe sweeping-on the shadeless noon,
>
> Were but my growing self, are part of me,
> My present Past, my root of piety.

(Sonnet Six)

Brother Isaac

Written in 1869, George Eliot's collection of eleven sonnets allowed her to reminisce about her time spent living in Griff House, and to recall the joy she felt when at play with her brother. There is a sense that the narrator of the sonnets, just like the poet herself, idolised her brother:

> If he said Hush! I tried to hold my breath;
> Wherever he said Come! I stepped in faith.

(Sonnet One)

However, the collection of sonnets does more than simply look back with nostalgia. They also look forward to a time of resentment and sorrow, when:

> the dire years whose awful name is Change
> Had grasped our souls still yearning in divorce
> And pitiless shaped them in two forms that range
> Two elements which sever their life's course
>
> But were another childhood-world my share,
> I would be born a little sister there.

(Sonnet Eleven)

In later years, despite their previous closeness, Isaac was never able to forgive his sister for her relationship with George Henry Lewes, whom she lived with outside of marriage. The narrator of *Brother and Sister* personifies Change as an unstoppable force of time and a strict observer of the damages caused by the siblings' opposing views. Change, therefore, is portrayed as a being which has the power to sever the once easy companionship between brother and sister. In spite of their separation, George Eliot hints that on either side there is a secret 'yearning' for reconciliation, but that both a difference in belief as well as the ongoing passage of time have now made this an almost impossible feat to accomplish. It is at this point that her sonnet is at its most autobiographical.

Before their separation, George Eliot and Isaac were apparently the closest of playmates, chasing around the grounds of Griff House and its surroundings, finding mischief where mischief was to be found, and entertaining themselves on the banks of the nearby canal. However, in reality, their relationship was much more complex and far truer to the relationships that typically exist between a sister and an older brother. Biographers have often commented on the paucity of information left behind by George Eliot about her time spent living in Griff House, and about her early years in particular. It seems as if throughout her life she made little mention of certain aspects of her childhood, even to those to whom she was closest. Many readers instead have turned to her fiction, and the depiction within her novels of childhood and the relationships children have with both their siblings, as well as their parents, in order to fill in the blanks about the early years of the novelist's life.

The Mill on the Floss

The Mill on the Floss has at its heart the relationship between the independent, intelligent Maggie Tulliver and her older brother Tom. It is the novel most scrutinised by readers keen to fill in for themselves the blanks regarding George Eliot's earlier childhood years spent living in Griff House. Victorian society dictated that, given the Tullivers' limited budget, as the only boy, Tom Tulliver must be the sibling sent away to receive the academic education that his cleverer and more determined sister seemed eminently more suited for:

> 'It seems a bit of a pity, though,' said Mr Tulliver, 'as the lad should take after the mother's side istead o' the little wench. That's the worst on't wi' the crossing o' breeds: you can never justly calkilate what'll come on't. The little un takes after my side now: she's twice as 'cute as Tom. Too 'cute for a woman, I'm afraid,' 'continued Mr Tulliver, turning his head dubiously first on one side and then on the other. 'It's no mischief much while she's a little un, but an over-'cute woman's no better nor a long-tailed sheep – she'll fetch none the bigger price for that.'
>
> (Book One, Chapter Two, *The Mill on the Floss*)

Mr Tulliver's discomfort that he should be burdened with a clever daughter, and his dubiousness as to the benefits of knowing a female with intelligence are a reflection of the beliefs of the age and nothing more. Indeed, he remains eminently fond of his daughter, telling her lovingly after she returns from some misadventures with a group of local gypsies,

> 'Pooh, pooh,' said Mr Tulliver soothingly. 'You mustn't think o'running away from father. What 'ud father do without his little wench?'
>
> (Book One, Chapter Eleven, *The Mill on the Floss*)

Scant evidence remains from Robert Evans' legacy as to whether or not he shared Mr Tulliver's misgivings when it came to considering the value of female intelligence, but given the emphasis placed on all five Evans children being educated, it would appear that this was certainly not the case. That a relationship of mutual warmth existed between George Eliot and her father also seems difficult to dispute. She was often permitted to accompany him on his horse and cart as he made his rounds across Newdigate land, her love of learning being nurtured by those times she was allowed to sit quietly and browse through the library at Arbury Hall.

Whilst there is little evidence to suggest that Isaac Evans shared Tom Tulliver's lack of ability, in many other ways the relationship between Tom and Maggie seems to have been a reflection of the relationship George Eliot shared with her own brother.

There is nothing to imply that Isaac was as unsuited for formal education as Tom, whose own father is heard bemoaning to his wife the fact that:

> 'what I'm a bit afraid on is, as Tom hasn't got the right sort o' brains for a smart fellow. I doubt he's a bit slowish. He takes after your family, Bessy.'
>
> (Book One, Chapter Two, *The Mill on the Floss*)

Maggie and Tom

Indeed, Isaac seems to have spent his time at school in a profitable way, at least as much as was needed to succeed in life. As his sister was to discover, he certainly assimilated and adhered to the strict moral code of the day, and he was for many years unrelenting in his determination to obey the beliefs he held so dear, displaying in particular an absolute abhorrence of couples who cohabited without having first been married. However, in many other ways, his youth suggests he shared some of Tom Tulliver's boyish tendencies. He enjoyed teasing his younger sister but, just like Tom, could tire of her extremely easily. When Tom is brought home from school by his father, his response to Maggie's greeting was no doubt a familiar scene that was played out several times in George Eliot's own childhood:

> Mrs Tulliver stood with her arms open; Maggie jumped first on one leg and then on the other; while Tom descended from the gig and said, with masculine reticence as to the tender emotions, 'Hallo! Yap – what! are you there?'

Nevertheless, he submitted to be kissed willingly enough, though Maggie hung on his neck in rather a strangling fashion, while his blue-grey eyes wandered towards the croft and the lambs and the river where he promised himself that he would begin to fish the first thing tomorrow morning.

(Book One, Chapter Five, *The Mill on the Floss*)

Although Tom makes it obvious that his first greeting is for his dog, Yap, and although he is all too soon considering what pursuits he shall be attending to, he does at least allow his younger sister to hang around his neck, perhaps revealing a subconscious tenderness for her. Indeed, later, Maggie's tendency to physically cling to Tom is a recurring image, and perhaps underlines her belief that of all her family members, he is the one who is closest to her, the one whose absence she misses most, simply because life is more bearable when his presence is near her:

Maggie's answer was to throw her arms around Tom's neck and hug him, and hold her cheek against his without speaking, while he slowly unwound some of the line, saying, after a pause,

'Wasn't I a good brother, now, to buy you a line all to yourself? You know, I needn't have bought it, if I hadn't liked.'

'Yes, very, very good…I do love you, Tom.'

(Book One, Chapter Five, *The Mill on the Floss*)

Tom has clearly understood his sister more than anyone else, for he has bought her a fishing line. Maggie does not yearn for bonnets, and she certainly does not concern herself with keeping them flat as Mrs Tulliver would wish her to. Instead, she prefers to be out of doors, tasting the freedom that, as a young girl, she is often forbidden from enjoying.

Mrs Evans

George Eliot was fortunate in that both Mr and Mrs Evans were in favour of educating their daughters as well as their son. It is possible, however, that there might be another reason for George Eliot and her sister Christiana (always known as Chrissey) being sent to school. Mrs Evans suffered from ill health. As the wife of a land agent who also took charge of his own land and farm, she would no doubt have been a busy woman. By the time she gave birth to twin boys, William and Thomas, in 1821, she was already a mother of three. Sadly, ten days after their birth, William and Thomas died. Mrs Evans was left exhausted and her health never recovered. There has been much speculation about the relationship George Eliot had with her mother, and in spite of the scant evidence remaining, the general conclusion seems to be that her mother's quiet, withdrawn personality created distance between herself and her children. This was no doubt deepened by her own ill health, which would have added further distance to their relationship. Indeed, it appears she found the presence of her stepchildren almost intolerable. Shortly after her marriage to Robert Evans, his son Robert was sent to Derbyshire to work, and his 14-year-old daughter Fanny went with him in order to be his housekeeper. Some critics believe this growing feeling of distance seems to have impacted upon her youngest daughter the most, perhaps, in part, because even at such a young age, George Eliot was aware that her sister Chrissey, quieter, and with less to say for herself, seemed outwardly at least to be her mother's favourite. However, other evidence points to this not necessarily being the case. After all, Chrissey was only young when she was sent away to Miss Lathom's School in Attleborough and even the school holidays did not find her back home at Griff House. Instead, Chrissey was more often than not sent to stay with her aunts (her mother's sisters), whilst Isaac was welcomed back at Griff, suggesting that he was the child who was most favoured.

Perhaps the most telling hint about George Eliot's relationship with her mother can be found in *The Mill on the Floss*. When Mr Tulliver loses his business and assets, Maggie burns with anger that her mother is more preoccupied with losing her dignity, possessions and social standing in the community than she is with the possibility of losing her husband:

> Maggie had witnessed this scene with gathering anger. The implied reproaches against her father – her father, who was lying there in some sort of living death – neutralised all her pity for griefs about table cloths and china; and her anger on her father's account was heightened by some egoistic

resentment at Tom's silent concurrence with her mother in shutting her out from the common calamity. She had become almost indifferent to her mother's habitual depreciation of her, but she was keenly alive to any sanction of it, however passive, that she might suspect in Tom. Poor Maggie was by no means made up of unalloyed devotedness, but put forth large claims for herself where she loved strongly. She burst out, at last, in an agitated, almost violent tone,

'Mother, how can you talk so? As if you cared only for things with *your* name on, and not for what has my father's name too – and to care about anything but dear father himself – when he's lying there and may never speak to us again.'

(Book Three, Chapter Two, *The Mill on the Floss*)

As her most autobiographical work, *The Mill on the Floss* seems to capture perfectly the tension that existed between Mrs Evans and her daughter. Both Maggie, who longs only to love and be loved in return, and her creator, are pushed closer to their fathers due to the distinct lack of warmth they are shown by their mothers, who either berate them, or are apparently preoccupied by other matters.

Mothers and daughters

Just like Dorlcote Mill, Maggie Tulliver's home in *The Mill on the Floss*, Griff House came with a large attic to which, as a young girl, George Eliot often escaped, enjoying the sense of freedom offered by its dusty spaces: its many heavy beams providing the perfect place on which to sit and daydream away the hours. In *The Mill on the Floss*, Maggie escapes the tortures of everyday life and the constant scolding of her mother by creeping into the attic at the mill and venting her frustrations on a fetish:

This attic was Maggie's favourite retreat on a wet day, when the weather was not too cold; here she fretted out all her ill-humours, and talked aloud to the worm-eaten floors, and the worm-eaten shelves, and the dark rafters festooned with cobwebs; and here she kept a Fetish which she punished for all her misfortunes. This was the trunk of a large wooden doll, which once stared with the roundest of eyes above the reddest of cheeks, but was now entirely defaced by a long career of vicarious suffering.

(Book One, Chapter Four, *The Mill on the Floss*)

Maggie would never physically harm her mother, so instead, she releases her pent-up frustrations on the fetish, driving nails into its head and 'alternately grinding and beating its wooden head against the rough brick of the chimneys that made two square pillars supporting the roof'. It appears that Maggie and her creator have much in common. Both grew up to be women ahead of their time after spending childhoods with mothers who found them difficult to understand. Similarly, both were sent away to boarding school only to have their education cut short due to family tragedy. Perhaps most important of all, however, is the fact that later, both would try to occupy a social space that was simply unready to receive them. Nineteenth-century society was no more ready for Maggie Tulliver's tangled relationships than it was for George Eliot's decision to live with a man outside of marriage. Both girls became independent women: seekers of freedom who challenged the patriarchy that blighted life for so many less brave than they. But thankfully for her many readers, George Eliot's life was shaped by a different course than Maggie Tulliver's, whose path was made worse by small-town gossip and scandal. Ultimately, their lives might have begun in a very similar way, but they ended in a completely different set of circumstances.

George Eliot was fortunate in that whatever distance she felt existed between herself and her mother, and whatever reason Mrs Evans may have had for not wanting her children beneath her feet all day, it did at least mean that all of the Evans children received an opportunity to be educated. When she was only 4 years old, George Eliot was sent with her brother Isaac to the dame-school opposite Griff House.

Education

Traditionally, dame-schools were run by women in their own homes. They were in essence a precursor to the nursery school, although the value of the education the pupils received could vary enormously from one dame-school to the next. Some dames offered little more than a glorified baby-sitting service, their own lack of education meaning that they themselves were unable to teach even the most rudimentary of skills. Other dames, however, were much more able, and did a good job of offering above par lessons in the basics of the three Rs: Reading, Writing and Arithmetic. It was not until 1880, and the introduction of compulsory education, that dame-schools were finally believed to be less than effective, and gradually, beginning with those of low standards, they began to close.

It seems, however, that the Evans children were fortunate in that the dame-school they attended, run by a Mrs Moore, was better organised than many. Mrs Moore was able to teach the pupils their letters and this prepared the siblings for their next stepping stone on the learning ladder. Isaac was sent to school in Coventry, whilst George Eliot was sent to join her sister Chrissey at Miss Lathom's school in Attleborough. This was the writer's first time she had been forced to spend a long period away from her beloved Griff House. At only 5 years of age she was rather young to be sent to boarding school, and this might account for the nightmares she began to experience. In later years she also recalled the bitterness of the cold that followed her around the school building, and her initial dread at being one of the smallest pupils, resulting in a constant battle for a place near the hearth so that she could at least enjoy some of the warmth of the fire.

There is no evidence to suggest that George Eliot was treated unfairly by her peers at school. Instead, her tendency to isolate herself, combined with her grave demeanour, caused them to call her 'Little Mama'. This was a different girl to the one who had left Griff House, and certainly there was nothing about George Eliot's attitude at Miss Lathom's to give the impression that she needed a fetish to wipe away her bad thoughts. Instead, as many young children do who are sent away, she developed a belief that she was to blame in some way for her departure from Griff House. As she withdrew further and further into herself, she found comfort in reading whatever literary material she could lay her hands upon. Moreover, she appeared to be older than her years, tending to prefer the company of adults, and she became determined to prove that if it was her bad behaviour that had resulted in her perceived banishment from Griff House, she was now a reformed character. If George Eliot hoped this would be enough to gain herself a reprieve, she was mistaken. Just three short years later, at the still tender age of 8, she was sent even further away to Mrs Wallington's school, The Elms, in Nuneaton, where she would join her sister Chrissey. However, whereas Chrissey, upon leaving the school, would in time go on to marry Doctor Edward Clarke, George Eliot's stay at The Elms provided her with something significantly different, and for a time sent her on the path to Christian Evangelicalism.

Chapter Five

In which George Eliot fervently embraces her faith before losing it, plunging her father into despair

Let my body dwell in poverty, and my hands be as the hands of the toiler; but let my soul be as a temple of remembrance where the treasures of knowledge enter and the inner sanctuary is hope.

(Daniel Deronda)

Miss Maria Lewis was the Evangelical principal governess of Mrs Wallington's boarding school in Nuneaton. Irish by birth, she was to be influential in George Eliot's life for the next fourteen years and even after the young George Eliot had left the school, Maria Lewis retained her influence through regular correspondence and visits to Griff House. That the Evans family approved of Miss Lewis is obvious from the frequency of her visits to their home. She was well-spoken and it was hoped by Mr and Mrs Evans that her quiet dignity would rub off on their daughter, helping to smooth any rough edges left over from a childhood spent mainly outdoors, often in the company of her brother.

Christian Evangelicalism

However, much more than good diction and a dignified manner began to influence the Evanses' daughter. She became enthusiastically devoted to her teacher's brand of Christianity, an Evangelicalism which was beginning to sweep across many parts of Britain, attracting those who were serious about their religion and who linked it, in particular, with the social and political climate of the day. Many Evangelists wanted to change society, although this meant they first needed to better themselves and renounce all sin. Evangelists believed firmly in the purity of the soul, so self-examination was a key part of their religion. Another key element was the strict observance of the Sabbath as a day of prayer. No moment of frivolity was to be allowed. Instead, Sundays were to be dedicated to Bible study and church attendance. The rest of the week was to be spent in pious sympathy of the religious edicts, and the indulgence of any type of pleasure was frowned upon. After such careful self-scrutiny, Evangelists were then expected to go out into society and perform good deeds. Among other things, this involved preaching to others about the benefits of prayer, helping non-believers find God, and visiting the poor and needy in order to bring succour and comfort to their lives. Thus, both the private and public lives of individuals were allowed to blend under the guidance of God and Christian Evangelicalism, a branch of religion which became so popular in the nineteenth century that it transcended both gender and class, meaning members of both the lower- and middle-classes became followers.

Robert Evans himself was inspired by aspects of evangelical Christianity, following a visit he paid to Nuneaton in order to hear some of the sermons given by the Reverend John Edmund Jones. Jones was a passionate speaker, used to evoking a variety of strong emotions in those who came to listen to his sermons, and the responses he elicited while preaching in Nuneaton were particularly powerful. Indeed, they led to several weeks of bitter quarrelling between those who supported Jones's beliefs and those who opposed them. The reactions he received were so strong that George Eliot later recalled them in *Janet's Repentance*, her short story from *Scenes of Clerical Life,* which depicts what happens in the town of Milby when an argument breaks out in the community between two very different factions of believers. On the one hand, there were the Evangelists, who could see the advantages of having the new curate, Mr Tryan, (based on the Reverend John Jones himself) join the parish, and so in turn were supportive of his appointment. On the other hand, there were those who remained in favour of the old curate, Mr Crewe, and were equally passionate in their defence of him remaining in Milby. In meeting places throughout the town, bitter and acrimonious disputes broke out between the two different factions, threatening to sever forever friendships that had previously seemed unbreakable:

> 'Well! I'll not stick at giving myself trouble to put down
> such hypocritical cant,' said Mr Tomlinson, the rich miller.

'I know well enough what your Sunday evening lectures are good for – for wenches to meet their sweethearts, and brew mischief. There's work enough with the servant-maids as it is – such as I never heard the like of in my mother's time, and it's all along o' your schooling and new-fangled plans. Give me a servant as can nayther read nor write, I say, and doesn't know the year o' the Lord as she was born in. I should like to know what good those Sunday schools have done, now. Why, the boys used to go a birds'-nesting of a Sunday morning; and a capital thing too – ask any farmer; and very pretty it was to see the strings o' heggs hanging up in poor people's houses. You'll not see 'em anywhere now.'

'Pooh!' said Mr Luke Byles, who piqued himself on his reading, and was in the habit of asking casual acquaintances if they knew anything of Hobbes; 'it is right enough that the lower orders should be instructed. But this sectarianism within the church ought to be put down. In point of fact, these Evangelicals are not Churchmen at all; they're no better than Presbyterians.'

'Presbyterians? What are they?' inquired Mr Tomlinson, who often said his father had given him 'no eddication, and he didn't care who knowed it; he could buy up most o' th' eddicated men he'd ever come across.'

'The Presbyterians,' said Mr Dempster, in rather a louder tone than before, holding that every appeal for information must naturally be addressed to him, 'are a sect founded in the reign of Charles I, by a man named John Presbyter, who hatched all the brood of Dissenting vermin that crawl about in dirty alleys and circumvent the lord of the manor in order to get a few yards of ground for their pigeon-house conventicles.'

'No, no, Dempster,' said Mr Luke Byles, 'you're out there. Presbyterianism is derived from the word presbyter, meaning an elder.'

'Don't contradict me, sir!' stormed Dempster. 'I say the word Presbyterianism is derived from John Presbyter, a miserable fanatic who wore a suit of leather and went from town to village and from village to hamlet, inoculating the vulgar with the asinine of Dissent.'

'Come, Byles, that seems a deal more likely,' said
Mr Tomlinson, in a conciliatory tone, apparently of opinion
that history was a process of ingenious guessing.

(Chapter One, *Janet's Repentance*)

The fact that these three men purport to be on the same side adds a touch
of gentle humour to this scene from the opening of *Janet's Repentance*. It
also makes readers consider the nature of the debate between Anglicans
and Evangelicals – when those who are meant to be on the same side in
this theological debate cannot prevent themselves from arguing, there
seems little to stop those on opposing sides from doing much worse.

Society and education

The debate between Mr Tomlinson and Mr Byles concerning the nature
of who, in society, should be educated, also touches upon an important
issue of the day. There were those like Mr Byles, who believed the 'lower
orders' were just as entitled to a rudimentary education as anyone else, in
spite of his lack of faith in Evangelicalism. Therefore, he disagrees with
Mr Tomlinson, who prefers to see boys filching eggs from nests than
embarking on a course of Sunday school study. This was an important
distinction at the time, as reading the Bible was particularly difficult for
those workers living in the countryside, many of whom had never had
the opportunity to be educated and therefore remained unable to read
and write. Dolly Winthrop, with her naïve yet honest and firm belief in
God, comes to exemplify this sort of Christian in the novel *Silas Marner,*
particularly in the scene where she tries to comfort Silas upon hearing
about the theft of his money:

> Dolly sighed gently as she held out the cakes to Silas, who
> thanked her kindly, and looked very close at them, absently,
> being accustomed to look so at everything he took into his
> hand – eyed all the while by the wondering bright orbs of
> the small Aaron, who had made an outwork of his mother's
> chair and was peeping around from behind it.
> 'There's letters pricked on 'em,' said Dolly. 'I can't read
> 'em myself, and there's nobody, not Mr Macey himself,

rightly knows what they mean; but they've a good meaning, for they're the same as is in the pulpit cloth at church. What are they, Aaron, my dear?'

Aaron retreated completely behind his outwork.

'O go, that's naughty,' said his mother mildly. 'Well, whativer the letters are, they've a good meaning; and it's a stamp as has been in our house, Ben says, ever since he was a little 'un, and his mother used to put it on the cakes, and I've allays put it on too; for if there's any good, we've need of it i' this world.'

'It's I.H.S.,' said Silas, at which proof of learning Aaron peeped round the chair again.

'Well, to be sure, you can read 'em off,' said Dolly. 'Ben's read 'em to me many and many a time, but they slip out o' my mind again; the more's the pity, for they're good letters, else they wouldn't be in the church; and so, I prick 'em on all the loaves and all the cakes, though sometimes they won't hold, because o' the rising – for, as I said if there's any good to be got, we've need of it i' this world – that we have; and I hope they'll bring good to, Master Marner, for it's wi' that will I brought you the cakes; and you can see the letters have held better nor common.'

(Chapter Ten, *Silas Marner*)

It was those people who shared Dolly's simplistic devotion to God that George Eliot began so fervently to disapprove of when she was at her most evangelical. Following the teachings of Miss Lewis, she came to feel that as a Christian, her role was not just to believe in God, but to preach about him to others, and to convert those not yet fortunate enough to have been touched by evangelical zeal. As an intelligent young girl on the cusp of adulthood, her beliefs went hand in hand with her keen, probing mind. For George Eliot, acceptance of an idea, an object or letters, simply because they appeared in the church, was not something she could comprehend; it was important that she knew *why* she was meant to cherish them and believe in their doctrinal goodness. As a simple woman who is able to admit to her own lack of learning, Dolly Winthrop is quite comfortable with the idea that if the letters I.H.S. appear in a church, then they must have their basis in goodness, and so regardless of her lack of understanding, she accepts they will imply mercy and charity.

Later in life, as the writer's religious beliefs changed, she herself came to appreciate the value that could be gained through simple faith. This is perhaps seen most clearly in her portrayal of Mr Gilfil in *Mr Gilfil's Love-Story*. Although as a vicar he is lacking in many of the skills that might be deemed important to the Evangelists – he preaches from the same batch of short, tired sermons on a rotation basis and shows little in the way of concern when it comes to educating his parishioners theologically – he is much more of a humanitarian, offering 'a great piece of bacon' to Dame Fripp when it becomes apparent that her pig provides her with so much company that she cannot countenance killing it for the purposes of enjoying its flesh. Indeed, following Gilfil's death, his flock show their warmth for him through the general mourning that takes place throughout the community:

> When old Mr Gilfil died, thirty years ago, there was general sorrow in Shepperton; and if black cloth had not been hung round the pulpit and reading-desk, by order of his nephew and principal legatee, the parishioners would certainly have subscribed the necessary sum out of their own pockets, rather than allow such a tribute of respect to be wanting. All the farmers' wives brought out their black bombasines; and Mrs Jennings at the Wharf, by appearing the first Sunday after Mr Gilfil's death in her salmon-coloured ribbons and green shawl, excited the severest remark…Even dirty Dame Fripp, who was a very rare church-goer, had been to Mrs Heckit to beg a bit of old crape, and with this sign of grief pinned on her little coal-scuttle bonnet, was seen dropping her curtsy opposite the reading desk.
>
> (Chapter One, *Mr Gilfil's Love-Story*)

Mr Gilfil's act of kindness in sending her some bacon had touched Dame Fripp far more than if he had tried to persuade her to sit through hours of religious readings, and the same could probably be said for most of his congregation. However, when she was a young girl, and at her most evangelical, George Eliot believed wholly in the importance of religious study and in the need for all Evangelicals to be learned enough to preach to their fellow man. As secure as George Eliot may have appeared intellectually, she was no doubt still insecure when it came to feeling appreciated and loved, particularly by her mother. Even though the years she spent at Mrs Wallington's boarding school were the years that shaped her, helping to cultivate her academic achievements, she was still aware of a distance and even a perceived coldness that existed in her relationship with her mother. Although we now know this can undoubtedly be attributed to Mrs Evans' feelings of exhaustion and illness, George Eliot was at an age when the support of her mother would have been very much needed, and the transference of her affection to the gentle Maria Lewis more than likely attributed to her zealousness, for in pleasing Miss Lewis, George Eliot was also trying to ensure that she was guaranteed some affection in return.

Academic achievements

However, in 1832, when in her thirteenth year, George Eliot's academic achievements could no longer be ignored, and Mr and Mrs Evans were advised that in order to benefit their daughter, they should send her still further away to Coventry, and to Nantglyn School run by Mary and Rebecca Franklin, the daughters of the minister of Cow Lane Baptist Church. At this school, George Eliot was subject to influences which were in many ways just as important as those she received from Maria Lewis, and which remained with her for the rest of her life. Most importantly perhaps, under the tutelage of Mary and Rebecca Franklin, she began to change the way she spoke, so that her voice was deeper and better modulated: the flatness of vowels beginning to disappear altogether. At Nantglyn, George Eliot was exposed to a more expansive curriculum, covering Literature, Maths, French and Music. She became accomplished at playing the piano, although she was often crippled by a lack of confidence when asked to perform in public, as is made obvious in a letter she wrote to Maria Lewis in 1838, when she had left the school and was almost 20 years old:

> I am not fitted to decide on the question of the propriety or lawfulness of such exhibitions of talent and so forth because I have no soul for music…it would not cost me any regrets if the only music heard in our land were that of strict worship.

Here, George Eliot's words reveal that her zealous nature and desire for 'strict worship' remained a constant in her life throughout her teenage years. It was while at Nantglyn that she also began to focus on her appearance, but not in the typical way that is often expected of young girls about to come of marriageable age. Already convinced not just of her plainness but of her ugliness, and certain that this was partly responsible for her mother sending her away and finding her difficult to love, George Eliot decided to cultivate a certain plain look. This idea of consciously forcing herself to accentuate the plainer aspects of her appearance, her long nose in particular, was to stay with her for much of her life, in spite of numerous efforts on behalf of other people to encourage her to take an interest in the way she looked. Whilst many of the other pupils at Nantglyn were beginning to consider the best way to appear most appealing in public, George Eliot became fond of wearing a plain little Quaker-type cap, which did nothing to enhance her features and everything to enhance those that others would have made every effort to hide. Her lack of vanity was puzzling to her schoolmates, who were now in awe, not only of her intelligence, but also of her religious views and her strict disregard of fashion and appearance in favour of fostering a simple, scholarly look for herself.

As Baptists, Rebecca Franklin and her sister Mary were quite mild-natured but, but never one to do things by halves, George Eliot adopted the most virulent form of the religion, ensuring that she prayed for perfection in herself, believing that fire and brimstone would be her misfortune in the afterlife if she behaved in a way that was anything less than saint-like. The weight she forced upon her shoulders was a huge burden to carry, and her need for perfection, driven by the promise of a cruel afterlife, must at times have seemed intolerable. Coupled with this was her belief that if she was as plain as she believed, she needed to make this her raison d'être in order to convince others that she was morally astute; whereas others thought of frivolities, she thought only of purity and piety.

However, beneath the unadorned surface she cultivated, there was a different side to George Eliot, and glimmers of this other personality appeared even while she was at school. The tears she shed over having to perform reveal that passion and anger did exist beneath the surface she presented to the rest of the world, and over her lifetime this manifested itself in the unrequited love from which she was to suffer.

Death of Mrs Evans

During the nineteenth century, many women also suffered through being forced to give up their education, their own ambitions – or at least those that society allowed them to have – in order to dedicate their lives to looking after elderly or sick relatives, or fathers left alone after the death of their wives. Being intelligent and academic in no way saved George Eliot from the same fate. In 1835 her mother fell ill with cancer, and by Christmas she was forced to give up the study that meant so much, leave the Franklin sisters' school and return home in order to help her sister Chrissey nurse their bed-bound mother. This was not the only fate that was to befall the Evans family, however, because not only was Mrs Evans dying, but just as her illness was reaching a peak, Robert Evans became sick with kidney problems.

Fortunately, in the twenty-first century, many kidney complaints can be easily cured, even if the pain of a kidney infection or kidney stones is not to be underestimated. However, in the nineteenth century, few remedies existed and the pain could be ferocious. It is surely a tribute to his stoicism and strength that Robert Evans emerged from the Christmas of 1835 alive, if weakened and less hearty than ever before. But worse was to follow. Over the next few weeks, Mrs Evans' condition drastically deteriorated, and by 3 February she had died.

This must have been an exceptionally difficult time for both George Eliot and her sister Chrissey, faced as they were with the inevitable death of one parent and the possible death of another. Even though the life of Robert Evans was spared, he was now a widower, used to the presence of a woman to keep the household in order, to organise the daily budget, meals, laundry and mending. There was nothing to be done but for the daughters to take over the running of the house and the care of their father, whether they wanted to or not. In the nineteenth century, little or no thought was given to a young woman's individual needs. Family demands came first, regardless of academic potential. If Robert Evans was going to continue with his work as a land agent and be able to keep Griff House afloat, his daughters would need to stand alongside him.

The fact that there appear to be no letters or journal entries from the time of her mother's death and father's illness is perhaps a testament to how very difficult this period in George Eliot's life must have been, especially for someone so prolific at both activities. Coupled with the grief she surely felt as a daughter – even more so considering their unresolved difficulties and the distance between them – there was also the bereavement that certainly would have been felt at her sudden loss of education and academic study. After all, for so long, such activities had filled the wide gap left by the lack of a mother/daughter relationship in her life. Now she was expected to leave behind something she was passionate about in order to replace the mother who had seemed so absent in her own childhood.

Self-education

In a trait obviously inherited from her father, George Eliot was nothing if not stoic, and so she gave up her school life in order to help her sister with the housekeeping duties at Griff House. However, there was, in time, some small compensation. In between fulfilling her duties as a housekeeper, George Eliot embraced one of the greatest cultural phenomena of the nineteenth century: self-education.

As someone who was used to the self-examination of Evangelical Christianity, and the Bible study that went hand in hand with prayer groups and theological discussion, the discipline of self-education came easily to George Eliot. Alongside her sister (before she left Griff House in 1837 to be married), George Eliot completed the duties that were expected of her. Like many young women in a similar position at the time, she attended church activities; visited the poor, the infirm and the sick; tended to her father; organised the household budget; paid visits that were deemed necessary to those in the nearby area; and generally completed all the chores, both large and small, however boring, that were expected of someone in her position. But her father's links to Arbury Hall meant that she was free to continue using its extensive study for personal use, and perhaps most importantly of all, Robert Evans allowed her to hire tutors from Coventry as a means of continuing her education. Whether this was due to the guilt he felt at forcing her to cut short her education, or because he sensed his daughter's frustration at feeling 'trapped' by organising household chores, when in reality she longed to pursue further academic study, it is difficult to tell. What we do know is that the lessons she received in music and languages added fulfilment to her life, and helped give shape to her private study.

Inner turmoil

As well as reading those classical texts that were believed to be suitable, such as the works of Shakespeare, Daniel Defoe, and Walter Scott, only the Bible and other religious tracts were initially on the reading list of a confirmed Evangelist. But inside George Eliot, a storm was brewing. There was a passionate side to this future novelist that, as she grew older, was not only beginning to make itself felt, but was also causing her to challenge all that she had previously held dear about religious doctrine and the need to lead as pure and pious a life as possible. The arrival of womanhood had caused her to question her constant need to remain on the sidelines when it came to experiencing life. The more invitations she received to parties and gatherings, the more difficult it became to sit and watch, like a spinster, when she had not even experienced anything of life for herself. It was as if she was made of two entirely separate beings. Half of the future novelist was a pious young woman, keen to expand her theological knowledge, and to prove her willingness to devote herself to religious doctrine. But on the other hand, part of her was impulsive and prone to passionate outbursts, such as when she was called upon to give a piano recital. As time progressed, it was getting more and more difficult to keep this part of her personality under control.

Much more significant than this, however, was the impact the depth of her reading was beginning to have on her Evangelicalism. The more she read, the wider the perimeter of her knowledge became, and the more inclined she was to challenge the beliefs she had held for so long. As she allowed herself to indulge in the reading of scientific and mathematical books, the more likely it became that the religious views she held, along with her adamant dislike of anything other than the staunchest of puritanical life choices, would begin to be called into question.

It was a decision made by Mr Evans himself, however, which precipitated the final relinquishing of George Eliot's beliefs. In 1841, Isaac Evans married Sarah Pountney Rawlins, the daughter of a leather merchant from Birmingham. That his bride was six years older than him was of little concern. What was of most importance was that in marrying Miss Rawlins, Isaac was linking his name with a successful, middle-class family from an affluent part of Edgbaston. In fact, it was at Edgbaston Parish Church that their marriage took place, with both of Isaac's sisters in attendance as bridesmaids. Chrissey was already married to Doctor Clarke and by nineteenth-century standards, George Eliot was fairly well taken care of and had only her father to attend to. In light of his son's marriage, and pleased with the young man his son had become, Robert Evans decided not only to give Griff House to Isaac, so that he and his wife could have the best start in life, but at the age of 67 he also retired, on the understanding that his job as land agent would be inherited by his son, whose whole education had been geared towards such an occurrence. With all these arrangements put in place, and after viewing a house at Foleshill in Coventry along with his daughter and Miss Lewis, and upon receiving their approval and being convinced himself of its suitability, the decision was made to move to Coventry.

Life in Coventry

Bird Grove, the house in Foleshill, Coventry, was set back from the road and situated in pleasant grounds. Although semi-detached, its Georgian architecture and design made it appear spacious and roomy. Indeed, in this regard its internal structure reflected its outward appearance. Bird Grove offered room enough for both Mr Evans and his daughter to live alongside each other without being on top of one another, and George Eliot was free to continue with her academic pursuits and her reading and letter writing with relative freedom.

Leaving Griff House, the only house she had ever known, after twenty-one years of memorising everything about its grounds, its attic and the people who lived and worked alongside it, must have been a huge challenge for the sensitive young woman George Eliot was known to be. That her brother was now the owner of the house probably made very little difference to her feelings, because it was now his wife who made decisions regarding housekeeping and interiors. In order to take her mind off such matters, George Eliot needed to keep herself busy.

Coventry in the 1840s was thriving. Its busy, industrial boom driven in part by the opening of the Coventry Canal, and then more importantly, by the beginning of one of the first railway lines between London and Birmingham, which ran through Coventry and opened in 1838. Coventry thrived in particular on its textile heritage. There had been silk weaving in the area since the 1700s, when the arrival of Huguenot refugees ensured that the area benefited from workers whose skills were predominantly in the weaving of silk and ribbons. Although the hand-operated looms, such as those worked on by Silas Marner, were originally used, they were later replaced during the Industrial Revolution by engine looms, which not only increased production greatly, but led to the employment of many people. Despite being just a short distance away, Griff House and the area around it must have seemed a world apart from the busy modern centre that Coventry had become. Bird Grove was similarly nestled quietly away from the heart of Coventry's manufacturing and economic centre and Robert Evans gradually grew concerned about the best way of launching his daughter into society, if that indeed had been his intention. With his son and other daughter married, it was only natural that the time seemed right for his youngest daughter to be presented to society, with a view to a gentleman from the right social class finding her suitable marriage material. It must have been difficult as a widower for Robert Evans to find ways to make connections in a busy place where he had few friends. However, he was nothing if not tenacious, and despite his advancing years, he did the only thing he felt comfortable with: he took his daughter to church.

There were plenty of churches in the area that Robert Evans could have chosen, the main one being Holy Trinity Church in the centre of Coventry. But if members of the Evans family were hopeful that this would be the perfect opportunity to introduce their spinster relative to a wider circle of families, and therefore a prospective husband, they were to be disappointed. George Eliot had already begun to feel the stirrings of religious disquiet that would stay with her for the rest of her life. This was initiated not only by the reading she was doing in her private study time – books such as John Smith's *Relation Between the Holy Scriptures and Some Parts of Geological Sciences* and Isaac Taylor's *Physical Theory of Another Life*, were examined and explored – but more importantly, a book called *An Inquiry into the Origins of Christianity* appeared on her desk, and was quickly read with much interest. Most importantly of all, however, and by strange coincidence, was the effect on George Eliot of meeting the author of the book himself and being introduced into his circle of friends.

That a struggle was going on inside George Eliot's head is obvious. Indeed, at times she must have felt tormented, torn as she was between the devout nature of the Evangelical Christianity which had played such an important part in her life during her formative years, and the new idea she was now faced with – that Christianity, like any other religion, was a subject to be studied, and that the Bible was a historical text to be analysed, deconstructed, and even doubted. When she had first arrived at Foleshill, George Eliot appeared to be a pious young woman, albeit one who was struggling with the serious aspect of her nature, but to her new neighbours, her devotion to her religion was never in doubt. This was particularly the case with the Evans family's immediate neighbours, Mr and Mrs Pears. The Pears family was already known to Robert Evans through his work as a land agent at Arbury Hall. Mr Abijah Pears was a prominent businessman and ribbon manufacturer, who was soon to be mayor of Coventry. His wife Elizabeth, however, had a particular reason for taking an interest in her neighbour's studious daughter.

Elizabeth's brother was Charles Bray, a ribbon manufacturer, and a brother-in-law of Charles Hennell, author of *An Inquiry into the Origins of Christianity*. She was highly concerned that her brother, a Radical, and his wife Caroline, also known as Cara, were beginning to turn their backs on Christianity, and embrace a life of Godless free thinking. Elizabeth hoped that by introducing such a religious young woman as George Eliot into their household, Charles and his wife might begin to have second thoughts about their Radicalism. She had no way of knowing that the young woman she believed to be so pious had already read Hennell's book, and was herself ready to begin to question her own devotion, turn her back on piety, and embrace a new world of free-thinking Radicalism.

Charles Bray

Charles Bray's wealth came both as a result of an inheritance from his father and from his hard work as a ribbon manufacturer. However, unlike many of the owners and bosses who benefited from the Industrial Revolution, Bray's interest in money was far from self-motivated. As a follower of the Welsh social reformer and textile manufacturer, Robert Owen, Bray believed in using his money to do good. Owen was a founder of the cooperative movement and inspired Bray with his efforts to improve some of the appalling workers' conditions he saw spreading across the country, mainly as a result of the Industrial Revolution. Owen was incensed by the greed that ensured some factory owners put wealth and income above the safety conditions and health of their workers. Robert Owen was also fascinated by the growth of socialistic communities, which he believed could be an answer to the rise of capitalistic greed.

Inspired by the works of Robert Owen, Bray began to use some of his wealth to effect change in a society with which he had gradually become more and more disillusioned. The gap between the richest and the poorest was growing ever wider and Bray despised the way that many of the wealthiest in society were willing to do nothing to close this gap in order to enjoy their privileges at the expense of the most vulnerable. However, Bray knew that if he was going to have any impact upon other members of society, he needed to gather around him a group of similarly like-minded people who were willing to address the same issues, and who were willing to try to convince others to believe the same.

Charles Bray and his wife Cara decided to use their home, Rosehill, as the perfect meeting place for those who wished to debate and engage in lively discussion about the current state of society, religion and politics. Robert Owen himself joined these gatherings, as did the American essayist and transcendentalist, Ralph Waldo Emerson. That the Brays were able to attract such a wide-ranging group of attendees is testament to how well-thought of they were in mid-nineteenth-century circles. Many of the visitors who attended the debates at Rosehill had one thing in particular in common: they either found it difficult to believe certain aspects of the Bible, such as the stories involving the more supernatural elements, for example, the parting of the Red Sea or the Miracles of Jesus, or they trod a very fine line indeed between atheism and belief.

Like George Eliot, Charles Bray had also experimented with Evangelical Christianity, and like her, had trodden the path of self-denying piety. But it was not a dalliance which had lasted particularly long. He was determined to find a type of religion which suited his personality and which, most importantly, did not bring self-sacrificing misery into his life. In Necessitarianism, he appeared to have found what he was looking for. Necessitarianism allows its followers to believe that God has already decided upon his laws; they are unchanging, and it is the duty of those who follow him to discover these laws for themselves. In the strictest sense therefore, the nature of possibility fails to exist, as everything has already been predetermined. Charles Bray was attracted to Necessitarianism because he believed it relieved individuals of the need to constantly attend a place of worship or follow a strict pattern of prayer. He saw that God was always right, therefore there was little need to pray to him, or to attend several services on a Sunday because the pattern of an individual's life had already been predetermined by an omnipotent God. Therefore, church was an irrelevance and the strict moral code of the Bible was outdated. Individuals should be free to enjoy themselves, to laugh on a Sunday and to lose their pious demeanours. No amount of prayer could change what had already been decided by God, so Bray believed individuals should spend their time more profitably, and instead of making a great show of going to church several times on a Sunday, they should look at how they could aid those in society who needed the most help, try to effect change where it was needed and be proactive in terms of charitable donations.

There is little doubt that this type of belief system appealed to George Eliot when she first encountered it. Firstly, it helped to free herself from the shackles of piety and self-denying sacrifice through which she had begun to feel so crippled. Secondly, it helped her deal with the religious doubts she had begun to experience: here was a way to allow religion into her life without feeling overwhelmed by it. Thirdly, and perhaps most importantly of all, by joining Charles Bray and his circle of friends, George Eliot was, for the first time, encountering a group of people with whom she could have the intellectual debates that had been missing from her life for so long. In perceiving Christianity and the Bible as an academic subject, instead of a fortress never to be penetrated or never once doubted, George Eliot was able to conceive of the idea of allowing religion to stay in her life, but very much on her own terms.

In his autobiography, *Phases of Opinion and Experience During a Long Life*, Charles Bray later recorded his memory of his first meeting with George Eliot, commenting:

> I can well recollect her appearance and modest demeanour as she sat down on a low ottoman by the window, and I had a sort of surprised feeling when she first spoke, as to the measured, highly cultivated mode of expression, so different from the usual tones of young persons from the country, we became friends at once.

His comment about friendship is an important one, because close friends would be something the young George Eliot needed in the following few months, when what she later came to call the 'holy war' broke out with her father.

The Holy War

George Eliot could not bear to be hypocritical, and once she had fallen into Charles Bray's way of thinking and believed in the importance of relinquishing regular church attendance, she refused to be seen in Holy Trinity Church or any other church in Coventry, not even for the sake of her father. Whatever Robert Evans' own religious beliefs may have been and however deeply they may have run, he was a man of tradition, and attending church on a Sunday was something that was simply done by all respectable families. He also began to enjoy his time attending various church services with his daughter. It was a way of making new acquaintances, renewing older ones, and as far as he was concerned, a way of helping his daughter to find a suitable husband. When she announced, therefore, at the beginning of January 1842, after keeping the peace over Christmas by attending church services, that she would no longer be accompanying him, his anger was palpable. He was also extremely confused. Still believing his youngest daughter to be as deeply religious as always, her new decision came as a great shock. He continued over the next few Sundays to attend church either alone or in the company of Maria Lewis, who no doubt felt helpless in the face of such father and daughter discord, and was concerned as to her old pupil's spiritual welfare. Robert Evans and his daughter lived in uncomfortable disharmony for two months, until on 28 February 1842, George Eliot took it upon herself to write her father a letter to try to explain her feelings exactly and to see if some compromise could be reached:

> Foleshill, Monday morning
> My Dear Father,
> As all my efforts in conversation have hitherto failed in making you aware of the real nature of my sentiments, I am induced to try if I can express myself more clearly on paper so that both I in writing and you in reading may have our

judgements unobstructed by feeling, which they can hardly be when we are together. I wish entirely to remove from your mind the false notion that I have any affinity with Unitarianism more than with other classes of believers in the Divine authority of the books comprising the Jewish and Christian Scriptures. I regard these writings as histories consisting of mingled truth and fiction, and while I admire and cherish much of what I believe to have been the moral teachings of Jesus himself, I consider the system of doctrines built upon the facts of his life and drawn to it as to its materials from Jewish notions to be most dishonourable to God and most pernicious in its influence on individual and social happiness. In thus viewing this important subject, I am in unison with some of the finest minds in Christendom in past ages, and with the majority of such in the present (as an instance more familiar to you than any I could name I may mention Dr Franklin). Such being my very strong convictions, it cannot be a question with any mind of strict integrity, whatever judgement may be passed on their truth, that I could not without vile hypocrisy and a miserable truckling to the smile of the world for the sake of my supposed interests, profess to join in worship which I wholly disapprove. This and this alone I will not do even for your sake – anything else however painful I would cheerfully brave to give you a moment's joy.

I do not hope to convince any other member of our family and probably not yourself that I am really sincere, that my only desire is to walk in that path of rectitude which however rugged is the only path to peace, but the prospect of contempt and rejection shall not make me swerve from my determination so much as a hair's breadth until I feel that I ought to do so. From what my Brother more than insinuated and from what you have yourself intimated, I perceive that your establishment at Foleshill is regarded as an unnecessary expense having no other object than to give me a centre in society – that since you now consider me to have placed an insurmountable barrier to my prosperity in life this one object of an expenditure held by the rest of the family to be disadvantageous to them is frustrated – I am glad at any rate this is made clear to me, for I could not be happy to remain as an incubus or an unjust absorber of your hardly earned gains which might be better applied among my Brothers and Sisters with their children.

I should be just as happy living with you at your cottage in Packington or anywhere else if I can thereby minister in the least to your comfort – of course unless that were the case I must prefer to rely on my own energies and resources feeble as they are – I fear nothing but voluntarily leaving you. I can cheerfully do it if you desire it and shall go with deep gratitude for all the tenderness and rich kindness you have never been tired of shewing me. So far from complaining I shall joyfully submit if as a proper punishment for the pain I have most unintentionally given you, you determine to appropriate any provision you may have intended to make for my future support to your other children whom you may consider more deserving. As a last vindication of herself from one who has no one to speak for her I may be permitted to say that if I ever loved you I do so now, if I ever sought to obey the laws of my creator and to follow duty wherever it may lead me I have that determination now and the consciousness of this will support me though every being on earth were to frown upon me.

Your affectionate Daughter, *Mary Ann*.

There is deep compassion behind the writer's words. In the articulation of her beliefs, George Eliot is understanding of her father's views and is willing to accept that the disharmony that exists between them might lead to the decision that his money is better spent elsewhere, rather than on paying for the upkeep of their Coventry house. She is honest about her feelings towards churchgoing and realises this might scupper any plans her father might have had for using this as a means of introducing her to potential husbands, in which case the money spent on Foleshill would not have been worth it. Her love for her father is something she refuses to deny, in spite of their differences, but regardless of her tenderness towards him, Robert Evans remained unmoved by his daughter's obvious distress. It was her brother Isaac who intervened on her behalf, inviting his sister to stay with him and his wife at Griff House until the immediate furore had at least blown over. George Eliot gladly accepted, no doubt happy for a chance to revisit the childhood home of which she had always been so fond, and relieved to have an opportunity to escape the frosty atmosphere that existed between herself and her father. Isaac's intervention might have been one of the reasons why Robert Evans, not a man known for changing his mind, did indeed make some moves to at least halt his intended course of action. The sale of Foleshill, which he had threatened to undertake, was for the time being postponed.

In her final novel, *Daniel Deronda*, George Eliot alludes to the discomfort that can occur when parent and child disagree, particularly when the disagreement is a serious one or involves a separation of some sort. In Book Seven, *The Mother and the Son*, the eponymous protagonist meets his previously unknown mother, Princess Halm-Eberstein, for the first time and is forced to listen to the disagreements between father and daughter which led to his adoption:

> 'I cared for the wide world, and all that I could represent in it. I hated living under the shadow of my father's strictness. Teaching, teaching for everlasting – "…This you must be," "…that you must be," – pressed on me like a frame that got tighter and tighter as I grew. I wanted to live a large life, with freedom to do what everyone else did, and be carried along in a great current, not obliged to care.'

This fictional conversation, and the princess's obvious frustration at what she perceived to be the marginalising of her world at the behest of her father, can be seen as a reflection of George Eliot's own feelings when faced with her father's apparent intransigence. Whilst determined to explore for herself more radical political, social, and religious issues, she believed his decision to cling to his own beliefs, and ensure his daughter did too, frustrated her future plans. It was this that ultimately led to the tension and separation between them.

Isaac's wife Sarah tried to intercede on her sister-in-law's behalf by visiting Robert Evans with a view to persuading him to show his daughter a little more leniency. Her intervention seemed to have influenced him somewhat. Interestingly, George Eliot was not abandoned by those friends she had made during her days as an Evangelical Christian. Her previous teachers, sisters Mary and Elizabeth Franklin, far from condemning her, tried to soothe Mr Evans' temper, and convince him that his daughter should not be disowned or sent away. Finally, after admitting to himself that he missed his daughter's presence, Robert Evans allowed her to return home. Similarly, she agreed to attend church with him, but made it clear that she resolved to maintain her own opinions concerning religion and worship. It was only when the pair were reunited that they were free to admit to themselves how much they had missed the company of the other. George Eliot's actions allow readers and literary historians to question her motives. As a seemingly independent woman, she might have made more of a claim on her determination to be free of religious ties. However, living once again with her father and perhaps colluding with a social framework she found difficult to disrupt, appears to have meant more to her than an outward show of rebellion. In short, there is evidence here of the social conservatism that George Eliot has so often been accused of displaying. For all her flashes of independence and strength, so uncharacteristic of the typically repressed nineteenth-century woman, George Eliot also believed that conflict for the benefit of individual glory should be suppressed and that instead, each person should look towards their own moral growth. She often reflected such ideas in her novels, particularly in the lives of her protagonists. Silas Marner, Janet Dempster and Dorothea Brooke are all characters who benefit from a quiet and subtle moral victory, rather than boasting of their strength or success through outward shows of glory or personal ambition. In spite of inspiring readers from all ages with characters who defied convention, George Eliot did so without being on a personal crusade to change society. Instead, her focus was always on the growth of the individual as opposed to the achievement of their personal ambitions. Silas Marner only achieves true happiness when his private ambition to endlessly work and earn money is replaced by his love for Eppie, and only when his need to help her draws him into community life does he finally secure true happiness for them both. He learns that there is something far more valuable than money and in due course, is able to enjoy the quiet tranquillity of personal happiness and the gradual fruition of community fondness:

In the open yard before the Rainbow the party of guests were already assembled, though it was nearly an hour before the appointed feast-time. But by this means they could not only enjoy the slow advent of their pleasure; they also had ample time to talk of Silas Marner's strange history, and arrive by due degrees at the conclusion that he had brought a blessing on himself by acting like a father to a lone motherless child. Even the farrier did not negative this sentiment: on the contrary, he took it up as peculiarly his own, and invited any hardy person to contradict him. But he met with no contradiction; and all differences among the company were merged in a general agreement with Mr Snell's sentiment, that when a man had deserved his good luck, it was the part of his neighbours to wish him joy.

(Part Two, Conclusion, *Silas Marner*)

These lines help to reinforce George Eliot's belief that attaining personal harmony and happiness is of greater importance than achieving the sort of inner glory likely to equip an individual to be an agent of social change. Silas Marner begins the novel as something of an outcast, and even when he moves to Raveloe he maintains his position as a marginalised figure, someone who inspires feelings of wariness and trepidation in others. However, life experiences teach him important lessons, and by the end of the novel he is surrounded by community love and care, is able to turn to his neighbours for help, or to look for friends with whom to celebrate life's quietly transformative moments.

Personal transformation

After moving back to Coventry and during the rest of the 1840s, George Eliot continued to go through the personal transformation which helped to shape the rest of her life. Her friendship with Charles and Cara Bray continued and her belief in their spiritual views remained undiminished. She spent a considerable amount of time at their house, Rosehill, and flourished while being allowed to question, challenge and debate the typical views of the day with other like-minded radicals, such as Harriet Martineau and the American essayist Ralph Waldo Emmerson.

Charles and Cara Bray were welcoming hosts to all of their guests, particularly George Eliot. In his autobiography, *Phases of Opinion and Experience During a Long Life*, Charles Bray reflected on his relationship with her:

> We had long frequent walks together, and I consider her the most delightful companion I have known; she knew everything. She had little self-assertion; her aim was always to show her friends off to the best advantage – not herself. She would polish up their witticisms and give them the full credit of them. But there were two sides. Hers was the temperament of genius which has always its sunny and shady side. She was frequently depressed – and often provoking, as much so as she could be agreeable – and we had violent quarrels, but the next day, or whenever we met, they were quite forgotten, and no allusion made to them. Of course we went over all subjects in heaven and earth. We agreed in opinion pretty well at that time, and I may have laid down the base of that philosophy which she afterwards retained.
>
> (p.73)

There are two ideas in particular which the reader is called to contemplate after reading this passage. The first is the depression George Eliot was prone to suffer throughout her life. Charles Bray's comments help to reinforce the idea that her moments of depression were very much exacerbated by those times when she felt listless, valueless or frustrated at having knowledge, but as a woman, having few places to share her thoughts. The conversations she engaged in at Rosehill did at least give her the opportunity to establish her opinion. Society was not ready for the original responses of a woman, and therefore her ideas stayed within her social sphere. Not even her family wished to converse with her on such matters, particularly when it came to religion.

The other interesting notion to arise from Charles Bray's comments is the nature of his relationship with the writer. The fact that he is struck by George Eliot's intelligence is obvious by his use of the word 'genius', but the reader might also wish to question how Cara Bray may have felt when she watched her husband and her friend sally forth on one of their 'long frequent walks together'. The answer to this question lies in the relationship choices made by the Brays themselves.

Charles and Cara Bray were nothing if not radical in their approach to life and therefore in their approach to their own relationship. Theirs seems to have been a marriage based on love, but also one based on freedom in that both husband and wife were able, by giving their own blessing to the other, to take a lover if they so wished. That they chose to do so within the confines of conventionality perhaps says something about how far they were willing to test the limits of a notoriously prudish nineteenth-century society. Or it could simply have been that they did not wish to draw attention to their particular situation so they could focus instead on the meetings at Rosehill. It was, after all, often easier to fight for radical change in the nineteenth century while apparently living by the very rules you despised. There is no evidence to verify whether or not George Eliot enjoyed both a physical as well as an emotional relationship with Charles Bray, just as there is little evidence to support the fact that Cara Bray had anything other than a deep emotional attachment to her particular friend, Edward Noel. But there is evidence aplenty to support the fact that Charles Bray and his mistress Hannah Steane were lovers in the form of the children that were conceived, one of whom, a daughter called Elinor, was later adopted by the Brays. It might be difficult for twenty-first century readers to condone Charles Bray's actions, which seem to scream of hypocrisy when we consider that he happily quoted from James Mill in his book *The Philosophy of Necessity; or The Law of Consequences as Applicable to Mental, Moral and Social Science*:

> The result to be aimed at is to secure to the great body of
> the people all of the happiness which is capable of being
> derived from matrimonial union...
>
> (*Elements of Political Economy*, p.78)

But it must also be remembered that Cara Bray herself appeared to be complicit in her husband's actions. Perhaps she felt their lawful marriage meant they were immune from public scrutiny and chastisement, a belief later borne out by the cooling of her friendship with George Eliot during the latter's enlightened relationship with George Lewes.

However, while she remained a frequent guest at Rosehill during the decade before she began living openly with Lewes, George Eliot continued to be on good terms with the Brays and benefited from their hospitality.

Das Leben Jesu

In 1844 George Eliot was asked to translate the German writer David Friedrich Strauss's *Das Leben Jesu* (*The Life of Jesus*) into English. The request came after a particularly turbulent time in her personal life. Although more content academically than she had previously been due to the reception she received from the Brays and their guests at Rosehill, nothing yet could convince George Eliot that she would ever be considered physically attractive, particularly when it came to the opposite sex. She still felt uneasy about her personal appearance and this tended to lead to her making significant errors of judgement. It perhaps came as little surprise to those who knew her well, therefore, when the writer began to exhibit signs of jealousy on meeting Cara Bray's brother, Charles Hennell, and the woman he loved, Elizabeth Rebecca Brabant. Intelligent, beautiful and known affectionately as Rufa, Elizabeth was blessed with coils of red hair which captured admiring glances whenever she was in company. In spite of the couple seeming ideally matched both in temperament and intelligence, Elizabeth's father, Dr Brabant, although an admirer of Charles Hennell's *An Inquiry*, failed to find much to admire in the text's author when he discovered he suffered from consumption. In the mid-nineteenth century, consumption shortened the patient's lifespan considerably, as well as weakening their constitution because there was no known cure other than regular seaside visits. This made Hennell seem a less-than-worthy groom for his daughter, and so Dr Brabant refused his daughter permission to marry. Nevertheless, the pair remained close and a wounded George Eliot was forced to watch yet another attractive couple fall deeper in love whilst wondering when similar attention might be paid to her. Having perhaps considered Charles Hennell as a suitable candidate for herself given her closeness to the Brays, all such thoughts were ended once and for all when Dr Brabant eventually gave permission for his daughter and Charles to marry. This undoubtedly had less to do with wanting to see his daughter happy in spite of her prospective husband's long-term illness and more to do with the fact that Rufa had lately inherited some money of her own, making her less reliant on her father or indeed her future husband should his illness worsen.

George Eliot was invited to serve as bridesmaid at the wedding, an action which no doubt reinforced her own position as an unmarried woman. There was, however, in her eyes at least, a consolation prize of sorts. The marriage ceremony allowed her to reacquaint herself with Dr Brabant, whom she was delighted to discover was excellent company. Dr Brabant, in turn, was obviously charmed by the much younger George Eliot, who apparently captivated him with her intelligence and open-minded thinking, so much so that he invited her to stay with him and his wife at their house in Devizes. If George Eliot was charmed by Dr Brabant, many other young women who encountered him were not. Indeed, Eliza Lynn, author of the novel *Lizzie Lorton of Greyrigg* and *The Girl of the Period: And Other Social Essays*, went so far as to describe Dr Brabant as 'antipathetic' and 'disgusting'.

A reader from the twenty-first century may wonder what drove a highly intelligent young woman like George Eliot to be beguiled by a somewhat unsavoury older man. After all, Dr Brabant obviously tried to unsuccessfully charm other intelligent young women who seemed to see through him. Ultimately, he was no more than a married middle-aged man who wanted to enjoy a short dalliance with a younger woman, regardless of her feelings. However, modern readers should perhaps remind themselves that George Eliot was at a particularly vulnerable point in her life. She feared that she was going to be left a spinster because of her perceived lack of beauty in a century which prized feminine charm and a woman's ability to marry above all else. Her intelligence and independence of thought did not make her entirely immune to the social mores of the day, nor in fact ignorant of her own desires and wants. Coupled with the hesitation still shown by her father to forgive her entirely for the change in her religious beliefs, it is perhaps understandable that she should form an attachment to an older man who appeared to understand her and, most importantly, accept her.

Life at the house in Devizes may have begun positively, but it ended on a rather ignominious note when Mrs Brabant made it obvious that

George Eliot had overstayed her welcome. Her husband revealed his weakness when he refused to support his guest and she finally made her return to Coventry. If she was hurt by Dr Brabant's failure to support her, George Eliot refused to show it. In fact, she threw herself into a project which only came her way because of her association with Dr Brabant's newly-wed daughter. Mrs Elizabeth Hennell had been commissioned by the MP Joseph Parkes to translate Strauss's *Das Leben Jesu*. However, married life and its domestic as well as social duties had taken their toll on Elizabeth, and she found herself too busy to complete the work. George Eliot, with her knowledge of the German language and her passion for intellectual and academic work, seemed the ideal candidate to undertake the commission. It was also felt by Cara's sister Sara Hennell and by Charles Bray himself that this work could be the very thing their friend needed to take her mind off all she had experienced over the previous few months.

Although it was the newly-married Elizabeth Hennell who had passed the commission of translating Strauss's work to George Eliot, she had not been the first one tasked with completing the work. Joseph Parkes had initially asked Sara Hennell if she would be willing to undertake the translation, but she had turned it down. She was, however, willing to act as George Eliot's editor, and ultimately each woman was given a role which not only gave them a suitable academic challenge, but which also allowed their friendship to develop and deepen.

It was not until 1846 that work on the Strauss translation was completed. The two years it had taken for George Eliot to complete her work proved to be academically taxing and the headaches which were to plague her throughout her life became a regular occurrence. One problem the writer faced was that some of Strauss's ideas challenged those she continued to hold, in spite of her otherwise less-than-orthodox Christian views. Although both Strauss and George Eliot believed that Jesus was a mortal human being, a man who captured the attention of people through his charismatic teachings, and not the son of God, unlike Strauss, George Eliot did not totally dismiss the New Testament. Indeed, she found much to admire in its positivity, and hesitated when translating Strauss's dismissal of this part of the Bible. Despite being bothered by such hesitations, Sara Hennell's role as editor had at least resulted in the two women maintaining close contact, meaning that when the translation was eventually finished, a celebration was very much the order of the day. George Eliot joined Sara Hennell in London, both translator and editor relieved that after all their hard work, *Das Leben Jesu* was eventually going to be published. At one point there were concerns that the translation might never even reach the reading public as it appeared that Joseph Parkes lacked the sufficient funds to bring the publication of the book to its fruition. When Parkes' concerns transpired to be real, help appeared in the form of John Chapman of London, who not only published *Das Leben Jesu*, but in doing so helped expose George Eliot to further academics, who would later become important to her when she was beginning her journey towards literary success.

Chapter Six

In which George Eliot not only faces loss and grief, but is also given some fine opportunities to travel

In the chill hours of the morning twilight, when all was dim around her, she awoke – not with any amazed wondering where she was or what had happened, but with the clearest consciousness that she was looking into the eyes of sorrow. She rose, and wrapped warm things around her, and seated herself in a great chair where she had often watched before. She was vigorous enough to have borne that hard night without feeling ill in body, beyond some aching and fatigue; but she had waked to a new condition: she felt as if her soul had been liberated from its terrible conflict; she was no longer wrestling with her grief, but could sit down with it as a lasting companion and make it a sharer in her thoughts.

(*Middlemarch*)

In 1845, Robert Evans broke his leg: the beginning of a succession of minor illnesses that weakened him and eventually led to his death. George Eliot was about to embark on a touring holiday of Scotland with Charles and Cara Bray when her father's accident occurred. Isaac wrote to inform her of events, but because the party never stayed in one particular place for long, his letter did not reach her for quite some time. In fact, the holiday was almost at an end before news of her father finally reached her. The Brays persuaded her to stay for one more day before returning with her to Coventry.

Robert Evans was in considerable pain due to his broken leg, but his daughter was also forced to acknowledge the seriousness of his general diminishing health. The breakage in his leg had undoubtedly weakened him, and so George Eliot was gratified to note that her presence seemed to brighten her father's spirits. However, together at Bird Grove, with only each other for company, Robert Evans' illness drew his daughter further away from the outside world and the liberal debates and academic conversations, which had allowed her to explore her religious and social ideas. Instead, she was forced to take up the role of sick nurse, attending to her father's every need. At first this was not so onerous a task. She enjoyed reading to him, and he took particular pleasure in listening to the Walter Scott novels, from which he had always derived so much joy. When he felt strong enough, there was still the possibility of travel to look forward to. She accompanied her father on holidays to Dover, the Isle of Wight and Brighton, and was able to take him on one last visit to Derbyshire, the county of his birth.

Although nursing her father could be tiring, it did at least give George Eliot an opportunity to experience once again the closeness with him that she had previously enjoyed. They talked and read together and for a time, frustrations regarding their different religious beliefs were put on hold. But other problems began to surface. As a woman with growing radical beliefs, George Eliot had enjoyed the invigorating talks and debates she had been allowed to participate in at Rosehill. Now that the frequency of such visits was severely curtailed, the narrowness of her life was exposed. It was made worse by the exhaustion she felt at having to accommodate her father's every demand. As much as she was willing to be a dutiful daughter, there is little doubt that caring for Robert Evans took its toll both mentally and physically.

This proved to be particularly the case the weaker her father became. Although he bestowed upon her much fatherly kindness during the months and weeks before his death – almost as if in expectation of his own demise – in his final days, George Eliot became more and more anxious at the thought of losing him. She had been most happy when his kindness gave her hope that their relationship had been repaired, previous disputes forgotten and he appeared to have months instead of just days of his life ahead of him. With the end of Robert Evans' time on earth so close, his daughter's resolve faltered as she prepared to lose the man who, in spite of their differences, had been the one constant male in her life. When she was young, she had put Robert Evans on a pedestal. His affection and understanding had replaced her mother's apparent disinterest. He had enabled her to be educated whereas other fathers simply neglected the education of their daughters. Instead, he had recognised her need for academic stimulation and sought ways of fulfilling that need. Her anxiety and sorrow in the face of her father's death can be seen most clearly in a letter she wrote to the Brays on 30 May 1849, informing them of the situation:

> Dear Friends,
> Mr Bury told us last night that he thought father would not last till morning. I sat by him with my hand in his till four o'clock, and he then became quieter and has had some comfortable sleep. He is obviously weaker this morning, and has been for the last two or three days so painfully reduced that I dread to think what his dear frame may become before life gives way. My brother slept here last night, and will be here again tonight. What shall I be without my father? It will seem as if a part of my moral nature were gone. I write when I can but I do not know whether my letter will do to send this evening.
>
> P.S. – Father is very much weaker this evening.

One of the things readers will note as being most striking about this correspondence is the way George Eliot breaks away from discussing mundane housekeeping details, such as Isaac's sleeping arrangements, to declare plaintively, 'What shall I be without my father?' It is an exclamatory remark to the Brays, suggestive of them being in the room with her more than mere recipients of a letter. This further underlines the despair she feels at the thought of her father's death, and highlights her feelings of loss and isolation at losing her moral compass, in spite of their past religious differences.

George Eliot did not have to wait long for the death of her father. The man who had been part of her 'moral nature' died that very night at the age of 76. He was buried a week later alongside his wife Christiana in Chilvers Coton churchyard.

It is Robert Evans' will which remains, to some, the most contentious part of his death. Indeed, to twenty-first century readers well-acquainted with both comparative equality between the genders and with the generally accepted idea of parents treating their offspring as equals, Robert Evans' decision to split his property and money in the way that he did remains perplexing. It is hugely important, of course, to bear social context in mind. In spite of how beloved or how needful a daughter may be, land was almost always bequeathed to sons. Robert Evans was certainly a man who believed in following the traditions of the day, so it no doubt came as little surprise to his family to discover that he had left his land to be split between Isaac, and his eldest son from his first marriage to Harriet Poynton, also named Robert. The split was an easy one to make. Land and property in the Nuneaton area was left to Isaac, and land and property in and around Derbyshire was left to Robert. However, when it came to bequeathing his money, Robert Evans seemed to be making a rather hurtful point with regard to his inability to forget the healing of old wounds. Chrissey and Fanny, the daughter he had shared with his first wife Harriet, had already received £1,000 each (equal to just over £100,000 in 2020) when they were married. Their father left them a further £1,000 apiece in his will, as well as some furniture. To George Eliot, the daughter who had looked after him in his final years and to whom he had been most close, he left £2,000 in trust (equal to £205,000 in 2020) and £100 in cash (equal to £10,000 in 2020). Perhaps what was most hurtful was the fact that he left his beloved collection of Walter Scott novels, not to his youngest daughter – the one who had been drawn closer to him once again through reading to him for hours as he lay on his sickbed – but to Fanny. No evidence can be found to show that Fanny had a particular claim over her father's Walter Scott collection, and so this act more than any other suggests that even on his deathbed, Robert Evans was unwilling to forgive the daughter who had looked after him so conscientiously because of their religious differences. The money she inherited from him also left her in relative poverty, particularly as unlike her sisters, she did not have a husband to support her. The £2,000 that had been left to her in the form of a trust fund was meant to pay her an income on a yearly basis and was to be looked after by her brothers. However, it would probably pay her less than £100 a year, and would therefore result in her living in reduced circumstances.

Freedom to travel

Evidence from George Eliot's letters reveals that she managed to live frugally on the money she was given, and therefore could begin to enjoy travelling further with the Brays in the hope of expanding her social circle, as well as her mind. She was still painfully aware of her status as a spinster, and it had been made obvious to her that now her father was dead, the rest of the Evans family did not need her. They had their own families to concern themselves with, and a spinster sister with apparently few prospects could be a burden. This would be particularly the case if she paid them a visit. She would simply be an extra mouth to feed, something Chrissey and her husband especially, even with Chrissey's inheritance, could ill afford.

George Eliot's sense of isolation at this time, in spite of her friendship with the Brays, could account for some of the rash and ill-advised decisions regarding romantic relationships she made in the following few years. In looking for someone to fill the gap left by her father, and in wishing to find a kindred spirit with whom she could spend the evenings in quiet companionship, reading and discussing the news of the day, George Eliot was sometimes known to exert a surprising amount of ill-judgement. This had happened previously, when her disappointment over Charles Hennell's marriage led to her unfortunate entanglement with Dr Brabant. Now, just days after her father's death, it was about to happen all over again with James Froude, the author of *The Nemesis of Faith*.

James Froude

Published in 1849 by John Chapman, *The Nemesis of Faith* was a novel which caused quite a stir with its Victorian readers. Telling the story of a young priest's struggle with his possible loss of faith, the novel's preface makes Froude's intentions clear to the reader:

> The moral of human life is never simple, and the moral of a story which aims only at being true to human life cannot be expected to be any more so. I do not think this book would have seemed so obscure as it appears to have seemed, if it had not been overly readily assumed that religious fiction

must be didactic. Religion of late years has been so much a matter of word controversy, it has suffered so complete a divorce from life, that life is the last place in which we look for it; and where I was painting a varying element in which a human soul was suffering and struggling, men have assumed that I was making a direct statement of my own opinions. I wrote a Tragedy...

It is easy to see the appeal Froude's novel held for George Eliot. When she first read it, she was interested in the idea of a man's faith being tested because of his doubt in the claims made by the Bible. Indeed, the novel's protagonist Markham Sutherland's belief that the Bible was based mostly on fictional tales passed from one person to the next seemed to complement George Eliot's fundamental idea that more historical fact would be useful in supporting the ideas and stories within the Old and New Testament. James Froude's message contained in the preface to his novel, that 'The moral of human life is never simple' would also have appealed to George Eliot at the time. She had first read and reviewed *The Nemesis of Faith* a few months earlier in the spring of 1849. Her father was already weakening at this point, and no doubt she was already concerning herself with how she would cope with the loss of her 'moral nature' upon his death. She was thankful that someone else understood the complexities of morality as much as she did.

In her review of *The Nemesis of Faith* for the *Coventry Herald*, George Eliot had been fulsome in her praise of Froude's work, commenting that while reading Froude's novel, readers:

seem to be in companionship with a spirit who is transfusing himself into our souls, and so vitalising them by his superior energy, that life, both outward and inward, presents itself to us in higher relief, in colours brightened and deepened.

James Froude was anxious to meet the anonymous writer of such a positive review, and was only able to surmise at her true identity because of a note she had sent him where she had referred to herself as the translator of Strauss. As both writers shared the same publisher, Froude was able to send correspondence to George Eliot through John Chapman, and she was excited to receive letters from a man she so admired. Unfortunately,

Froude's first visit to Rosehill came at a less than propitious time. Not only did he arrive shortly after Robert Evans' burial, when George Eliot was at her most fragile both physically and mentally, but his visit also clashed with the tumult of packing for an overseas trip. In order to aid her recovery from the last few months, the Brays were taking their friend on a European tour. The couple had the idea that asking Froude along on their holiday might help with her recovery, and Cara was particularly hopeful that out of the pain of the last few months, romance might blossom. Froude accepted the invitation and there was much happiness all round.

However, the morning of the tour brought bad news. Just as the travellers from Rosehill were boarding a train, John Chapman came hurtling down the platform, desperate to catch them before their train left the station for Folkestone. The news he had to deliver should, by rights, have been brought by James Froude, but it seemed the writer was not brave enough to speak for himself so he sent his publisher on his behalf. John Chapman explained to the puzzled party of three that Froude would not be joining them after all. Instead, he was to be married in a few weeks' time. If the news came as a huge shock to the Brays, it came as an even greater one to George Eliot, and hurt her considerably. She had just gone through one of the most difficult times of her life so far, only to be faced with the embarrassment of further rejection. It remains a mystery as to why Froude was not more honest in the first place. When he agreed to go on the European tour, he must have known he was engaged to be married. One theory could be that he was delaying a possible proposal until he had met the translator of Strauss for himself. But once he had met her and appreciated her physical charms did not match her academic ones, and that her intelligence was not equalled by her beauty, he decided to pursue his original fiancée and was simply too embarrassed to refuse the offer of a European tour when it was made to him. When he realised he needed to inform the Brays and George Eliot of his decision and the reason behind it, he saved himself any awkwardness by sending John Chapman in his place.

Whatever James Froude's reasons were for changing his mind, the impact on an already vulnerable George Eliot remained the same. Already mourning the death of her father, her loss and isolation, in spite of having the Brays as travelling companions, seemed to emphasise even further her position as a spinster. After all, she would have reasoned to herself, the Brays were married and she was not. However unconventional their marriage might be if judged within the confines of nineteenth-century standards, Cara and her husband would always have each other to rely upon in times of a crisis. George Eliot believed she would have no-one and her feelings of solitude continued to haunt her throughout her European tour.

It must have been a difficult holiday for the Brays and no doubt it put a strain upon them. Here they were having the good fortune to travel through such places as Paris and Genoa, when all the time their excitement was being kept in check by their companion's tearful demeanour. Their final destination was Geneva, and it was here that things changed for all three travellers. George Eliot had always felt the Swiss city would be a delightful place to take up residence. It was the birthplace of Jean-Jacques Rousseau, a writer and philosopher she admired greatly. Along with the knowledge that she still had the £100 in cash inherited from her father, she decided to spend some time alone in a Genevan pension, determined that such a break would lighten her spirits and bring some joy back into her life. After spending a few short days in Geneva, the Brays returned to the normality of their life in Coventry, leaving their friend to begin her new one in a strange city.

Life in Geneva

Tourism in Geneva was beginning to flourish during the nineteenth century. Although the Grand Tours of wealthy, upper-class young men of the seventeenth and eighteenth centuries had already afforded a certain class and gender the opportunity of cultural travel, the dawn of the nineteenth century broadened such opportunities for women as well as the middle-classes. The travel companies Thomas Cook and Lunn Travel were the first groups to offer officially organised tourist holidays to Switzerland in the 1800s. There was little chance, therefore, that George Eliot would find herself alone when she stayed in Geneva unaccompanied, for the first time. However, one difficulty she did encounter was that many of the people she met were short-stay tourists simply passing through Geneva, making it increasingly difficult for her to make friendships that would last throughout her sojourn. Another difficulty was the fact that she had no chaperone. In her home town of Coventry, indeed, throughout any town or city in Britain, an unmarried woman who had turned 30 would have been able to walk alone with relative freedom – her role as a spinster being more or less confirmed – so that society would consider her out of danger from the molestations of men and she would therefore be unlikely to sully her innocence and good name. The same beliefs tended not to exist in mainland Europe, where single women in their thirties and forties were still considered to need protection. George Eliot was therefore confined to her pension more days than she would have liked.

However, her readers have one particular reason to be thankful for her time spent in Geneva. The many letters she filled her time with writing helped to develop her skill for noticing the tiny, intricate details that would later furnish her future novels with so much realism. George Eliot was able to watch the quirks and conceits of her fellow travellers and commit them to paper in the letters she wrote in order to entertain her correspondents, such as Charles and Cara Bray, her brother Isaac, and her sisters Fanny and Chrissey. Unfortunately, her own sense of isolation was to be further reinforced by the lack of letters she received in return, and this only fuelled her grief and loss. With their friend away from Coventry, no doubt the Brays thought it was an ideal opportunity to escape for a time from the sadness they had been surrounded by while in her company. Perhaps they also felt tired of her constant moaning and complaining. However, in spite of her grief, George Eliot was still able to include witty and colourful descriptions of her fellow guests in her letters:

> I have made another friend too – an elderly English lady,
> a Mrs Locke, who used to live at Ryde – a pretty old lady,
> with plenty of shrewdness and knowledge of the world. She
> began to say very kind things to me in rather a waspish tone
> yesterday morning at breakfast. I liked her better at dinner
> and tea, and today we are quite confidential.
>
> (Letter to the Brays, 27 July 1849)

But she was also capable of moaning, griping and belittling herself as usual:

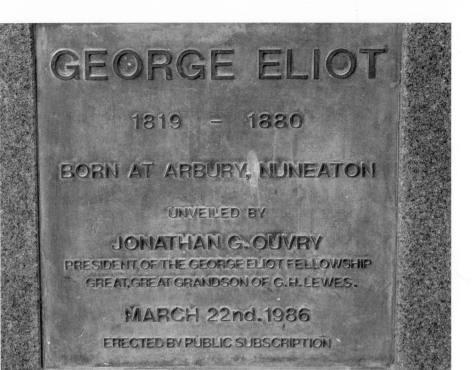

Inscription on the front of George Eliot's statue in Nuneaton giving details of the unveiling.

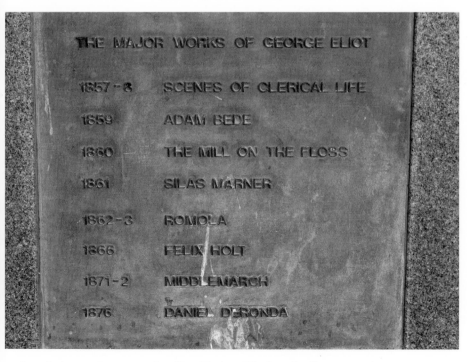

Inscription on the statue, detailing George Eliot's major literary works.

Inscription on the George Eliot statue, Nuneaton.

MARY ANN EVANS (GEORGE ELIOT).
NOVELIST, ESSAYIST, JOURNALIST AND POET
LIVED AT GRIFF HOUSE UNTIL 1840 WHEN SHE
MOVED TO COVENTRY AND LATER TO LONDON.

FROM 1854 TO 1878 SHE LIVED WITH G.H. LEWES
WHO ENCOURAGED HER TO WRITE FICTION. HER
NOVELS BROUGHT HER WORLD WIDE FAME.

IN MAY 1880 SHE MARRIED J.W. CROSS AND DIED
IN DECEMBER AT 4 CHEYNE WALK, CHELSEA.

SHE IS BURIED IN HIGHGATE CEMETERY, LONDON.

Further inscription on the George Eliot statue.

Above: The front view of the
George Eliot Hotel, Nuneaton.

Right: The George Eliot Hotel,
Nuneaton.

Left: The main entrance to St Nicolas church, Nuneaton. The church was the inspiration for Milby Church in *Scenes of Clerical Life*.

Below: St Nicolas church, Nuneaton.

Nuneaton Museum and Art Gallery.

A front view of the Round Towers, Arbury. Arbury Hall was the ancestral home of the Newdigate family and Robert Evans (George Eliot's father) worked on the Arbury Estate.

Left: The Round Towers, Arbury.

Below: The grounds of Astley Castle. The castle was the inspiration for Knebley Manor which appeared in *Scenes of Clerical Life*.

Above: A side view of Astley Castle.

Right: Interior of Astley church.

Astley Castle.

Astley Castle and grounds.

An information board at Astley, including a picture of George Eliot in the top right corner.

George Eliot (1819-1880)

During the 19th century, Astley inspired the writer George Eliot. She was born Mary Anne Evans and grew up on the Arbury Estate, where her father was a land agent. When she became a writer, Mary Anne took a man's name to ensure her works were taken seriously. She is one of the greatest 19th-century novelists.

Astley is said to be the model for 'Knebley' in *Scenes of Clerical Life* (1857). Eliot drew inspiration for several of her characters from those she grew up with.

"*...a wonderful little church with a chequered pavement which had once rung to the iron trod of military monks, with coats of arms in clusters on the lofty roof, marble warriors and their wives without noses...and the twelve apostles, with their heads very much on one side, holding didactic ribbons, painted in fresco on the walls.*"

Scenes of Clerical Life, Mr Gilfil's Love Story

An information board at Astley, including an image of George Eliot.

Right: A side view of Astley church.

Below: Astley church.

Information board at Astley.

Griff House, George Eliot's childhood home, which is now a Beefeater pub.

Griff House: the sash windows help the pub retain its link to the past.

Griff

Until the 21st century the hamlet of Griff remained a tiny enclave of the original parish of Chilvers Coton.

Thatched houses and cottages, an ancient pub, old pit tips, remains of waterways which formerly connected up to the Arbury estate, serve as a reminder of its former days. A large house now a hotel, Griff House was where Henry Beighton, who made the first 1¼ mile map of Warwickshire, lived in the early 18th century. It was later the home of George Eliot.

The round pond which featured in "Mill on the Floss" still remains in the grounds close to Coton Farm.

The site of Griff (Sudeley Castle) Manor House is now buried under the large island at the junction of the A444 and other roads. In about 1154 Ralph de Sudeley gave land to found a priory which is now under Arbury Hall and also laid in the vicinity of Bermuda Village to the Knights Templar in 1185. The manor house was decorated by 1182.

At Griff Lodge Farm part of the building dates back to 1642. Griff Lodge is one of three entrances to Arbury Hall, built in 1584. The hall was gothicised by Sir Roger Newdigate's day.

Arbury Mill was built in the late 17th or early 18th century. It was recalled as the "Mill on the Floss" by George Eliot.

Along the road to Bedworth there is a thatched Cottage. This has been completely renovated.

It dates back to the early 1600's. It is often referred to "Bob Jakin's Cottage" after a character in George Eliot's "Mill on the Floss".

The Griffin Inn dates back to 1654.

Mining began in the area in 1329 and in 1714 one of the first Newcomen-Savery Beam Engine was installed at Griff, Little Brace Pit.

The Arbury Communication canal was opened in August 1771.

A horse-drawn tramway, built in 1819, connected outlying pits to a wharf on the Arbury Communication Canal.

BERMUDA VILLAGE

Bermuda village was built in 1891. It was so named because Lieutenant General Sir Edward Newdigate - Newdegate was Governor of Bermuda between October 1888 and June 1891.

NOTABLE GRIFF PEOPLE
GEORGE ELIOT (1819-1880)

The Victorian novelist was born Mary Ann Evans at South Farm on the Arbury estate on 22nd November 1819. She moved with her father Robert Evans (1773-1849) to Griff House early in 1820. Her first series of novellas "Scenes of Clerical Life" were serialised by William Blackwood in 1857. These were thinly disguised episodes and events about the local people she knew in Chilvers Coton, Nuneaton and on the Arbury estate during her formative years.

HENRY BEIGHTON (1687-1743)

Henry Beighton, Fellow of the Royal Society, surveyor and engineer, was born and lived the whole of his life in the parish of Chilvers Coton, in the Hamlet of Griff. He developed the modern method of recording meteorology and weather science. He was a brilliant cartographer, and has been described as the "Father of Modern Map-making". He was also Editor of the "Ladies Diary". He illustrated Thomas's edition of Sir William Dugdale's "Antiquities of Warwickshire". He lived at Griff House (the original demolished) and later at a house called "Barracks" now demolished.

The Griff Arm of the Coventry Canal c.1900.

Griff House. Mary Ann Evans lived here 1820-1841.

Griff House in 2005 is a modern hotel and restaurant.

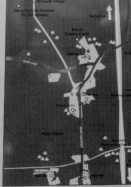
Map of Griff Area c.1908.

Information relating to Griff House.

Above: View of Tenby as it is today.

Left: Signage displayed on the guesthouse in Tenby where George Eliot stayed.

WHILE ON HOLIDAY HERE
MARY ANN EVANS
WAS INSPIRED TO WRITE HER FIRST
NOVEL PUBLISHED IN 1857
UNDER THE NAME OF
GEORGE ELIOT

Above: A view of the row of guesthouses where George Eliot stayed in Tenby.

Right: Many of the streets in Tenby are narrow and just as they would have appeared in the nineteenth century.

A Tenby street near to where George Eliot stayed, still with its original street lamp.

All the world says I look infinitely better; so I comply, though to myself I look uglier than ever – if possible. I am fidgeted to death about my boxes, and that tiresome man not to acknowledge the receipt of them.

(Letter to the Brays, 20 August 1849)

Constantly describing such miserable thoughts in her letters, even while staying in the city she had always dreamed of visiting, could be irksome to the recipients, especially as the Brays probably thought they had already done a considerable amount in the name of friendship.

However, there seems to be little reason for her siblings to pay such scant regard to their sister during her time abroad. They must have realised how lonely she would feel while living in a country that was quite new to her, and how unhappy she must have felt while still grieving for the loss of their father. Yet in spite of this, the letters to arrive from home were few and dated many months apart.

In spite of the lack of correspondence from both friends and family, George Eliot continued to pen highly-detailed letters. In this way, not only was she able to pass the time when feeling unable to leave the pension, but she was also able to keep a specific audience entertained with her thoughts and observations. In a letter to the Brays dated 28 August 1849, George Eliot wrote with surprising positivity and in doing so, she created a charmingly detailed picture of life in Geneva and, most importantly, of the people with whom she became acquainted.

Mme de Ludwigsdorff, the wife of an Austrian baron, has been here for two days, and is coming again. She is handsome, spirited and clever – pure English by birth, but quite foreign in manners and appearance. She, and all the world besides, are going to winter in Italy. Nothing annoys me now, – I feel perfectly at home, and shall really be comfortable when I have all my little matters about me. This place looks lovely to me every day, – the lake, the town, the compagnes with their stately trees and pretty houses, the glorious houses in the distance; one can hardly believe oneself on earth: one might live here and one might forget that there is such a thing as want or labour or sorrow. The perpetual presence of all this beauty has somewhat the effect of mesmerism or chloroform. I feel sometimes as if I were slipping into an agreeable state of numbness on the verge of consciousness, and seem to want well pinching to rouse me. The other day (Sunday) there was a fete held on the lake – the fete of Navigation. I went out with some other ladies in M de H's boat at sunset, and had the richest drought of beauty. All the boats of Geneva turned out in their best attire. When the moon and stars came out there were beautiful fireworks sent up from the boats. The mingling of the silver and golden rays on the rippled lake, the bright colours of the boats, the music, the splendid fireworks, and the pale moon looking at it all with a sense of grave surprise, made up a sense of perfect enchantment, and our dear old Mont Blanc was there in his white ermine robe.

Such beautiful detail surely prepared her for writing some of the descriptive passages which appeared in *The Mill on the Floss* almost eleven years later, when in Book Two Chapter Two she captured the natural charms of winter:

Snow lay on the croft and river-bank in undulations softer than the limbs of infancy; it lay with the neatliest finished border on every sloping roof, making the dark-red gables stand out with a new depth of colour; it weighed heavily on the laurels and fir-trees till it fell from them with a shuddering sound; it clothed the rough turnip-field with whiteness and made the sheep look like dark blotches; the gates were all blocked up with the sloping drifts, and here and there a disregarded four-footed beast stood as if petrified 'in unrecumbent sadness'; there was no gleam, no shadow, for the heavens too were one still pale cloud – no sound or motion in anything but the dark river, that flowed and moaned like an unresting sorrow.

George Eliot's ability to bring nature to life, to bestow upon it touches of humanity, is something which characterises her writing throughout her career. The letters she wrote from Geneva gave her the opportunity to hone her descriptive and narrative skills in readiness for writing the novels she lacked the confidence to commit to so early on in her writing career.

Despite her letter of 28 August apparently suggesting she was finally happy and well settled in the Genevan pension, George Eliot had actually grown tired of life among the ever-changing flow of tourists. She found that even those like herself – who were longer-staying guests – could easily irritate and annoy her. She was not a woman to enjoy spending an evening gossiping about other residents, and unfortunately, she discovered that many of the people who drifted through the sitting rooms of the pension enjoyed passing the time by doing exactly that. Finding herself growing increasingly unsettled, a solution appeared in the home of François D'Albert Durade and his wife, where she would be able to stay as the sole paying guest. In a letter to the Brays dated 4 October 1849, she wrote:

> I am anxious for you to know my new address as I shall leave here on Tuesday. I think – I have at last found the very thing. I shall be the only lodger. The apartment is *assez joli* with an alcove, so that it looks like a sitting room in the day-time – the people, an artist of great respectability and his wife, a most kind-looking, lady-like person, with two boys who have the air of being well-educated. They seem very anxious to have me and are ready to do anything to accommodate me. I shall live with them – that is dine with them; breakfast in my own room. The terms are 150 francs per month, light included. M and Mme D' Albert are middle-aged – musical and I am told have *beaucoup d'esprit*. I hope this will not exceed my means for four or five months. There is a nice large salon and a good *salle a manger*. I am told that their society is very good. Mme de Ludwigsdorff was about going there a year ago and it was she who recommended it to me.

In a later letter written to the Brays on 26 October 1849, George Eliot continued to be fulsome in her praise of her hosts. Of Monsieur D'Albert Durade she wrote:

> One feels a better person when he is present. He sings well, and plays on the piano a little. It is delightful to hear him talk of his friends – he admires them so genuinely – one sees

so clearly that there is no reflex egotism. His conversation is charming. I learn something every dinner time.

And of his wife, she wrote the following:

Mme D'Albert has less of genius and more of cleverness – a real lady-like person who says everything well. She brings up her children admirably – two nice intelligent boys – the youngest particularly has a sort of Lamartine expression with a fine head. It is delightful to get among people who exhibit no meanness, no worldliness, that one may well be enthusiastic.

François D'Albert Durade was a Swiss national born in 1804. Hurt in an accident in his youth, he was particularly short for a man and had a deformed spine. Although George Eliot was to describe him as 'plain', nothing in his portrait suggests he had anything other than a kindly and expressive face. He and his wife were undoubtedly a charismatic, warm and generous couple, who enjoyed patronising the arts and engaging in interesting literary conversations. However, they were also the type of people who could easily, albeit inadvertently, draw the vulnerable and still grieving George Eliot much closer to them than they might have wanted. It was not long, therefore, before their paying guest was becoming much more embroiled in their domestic life than was healthy for any of them.

There is little doubt that Monsieur D'Albert Durade was particularly taken with George Eliot, and the familiar pattern which had begun to play out during her visit to Dr Brabant began to repeat itself all over again. The pair began to spend a considerable amount of time together, to the exclusion of the rest of the household. They especially enjoyed reading, discussing art and literature, and walking. Durade even went so far as to suggest that his guest sit for him while he painted her. It is interesting to consider how the artist's wife felt about the number of hours her husband spent with their paying guest, particularly as she was left alone to occupy their two sons. As the year drew to a close and 1850 dawned, however, there was little sign that Madame Durade begrudged her husband and guest the time they spent in each other's company. Indeed, the status quo did not change until the spring, with George Eliot's sudden decision, several months early, to return home. Although there had been plans for Monsieur Durade to accompany her to Paris in order to engage in some sightseeing, this was abandoned, it being deemed too expensive a trip. Instead, it was decided that the pair would journey together to London, allowing Durade time to indulge his passion for art in the galleries there, before accompanying his companion to Coventry and then returning home.

It is easy to speculate upon the reasons why George Eliot returned from Geneva earlier than planned. Certainly, life with the Durades offered her the opportunity to engage with all the activities she longed to be part of, the musical evenings, for example, the debates and artistic gatherings that she had dreamed about and which had disappointingly been missing at the pension. Life with Monsieur Durade and his wife had provided George Eliot with the same stimulating conversation that she thrived on at the Brays, but just as she had been tempted to fall in love with Charles Hennell, and put herself in danger of being taken advantage of by Dr Brabant, now she was in jeopardy of becoming too attached to Monsieur Durade. Perhaps George Eliot sensed this and decided to put some distance between herself and the artist, or perhaps Madame Durade decided it was time for their English guest to return home before attachments grew too deeply. Either way, by the middle of March, George Eliot, accompanied by Monsieur Durade, set out for England and several days spent visiting the art galleries of London. After leaving his charge at Rosehill, Monsieur Durade returned home to his wife and family. However, his friendship with George Eliot did not end there. The two maintained a lasting correspondence which unfortunately cannot add to the readers' knowledge of their relationship. Upon her death, Durade destroyed all of the letters he had received from her, so their feelings for each other can never truly be known. The fact that he translated several of her novels into French suggests it was amicable at the very least.

When she finally returned to Coventry, George Eliot was forced once again to re-evaluate her life! It became more than clear to her, after visiting her siblings, that with the exception of Chrissey, who remained kind and gentle, none of her other family members could spare her the time she needed to recover from the loss of their father. She was not making any money from her writing, she had no husband to support her and the only role she considered herself to have completed successfully by the time she was 30 was that of nurse-maid. It is little wonder, therefore, that she believed the only course of action available to her was to find employment as a carer. But it became obvious to her very quickly that she was not needed in the household of any family member. Feeling ostracised and alone, she struggled to find a place to call home until she was struck with an interesting idea. She would move to London.

London life

London in 1850 was a city of very mixed fortunes. Those with money could afford to live in houses away from the squalor of the inner-city slums, with their poverty, crime and disease-ridden streets. The gap between rich and poor was an ever-widening one as the nineteenth century progressed, in spite of the fact that by the middle of the 1800s, London was one of the world's wealthiest cities. However, all the money in the world could apparently do nothing to save the jewel in Britain's crown from the rampant problem of over-crowding. With more and more people moving to the capital looking for work, its streets soon became filled to the brim with those desperate for a place to live. The result of this was that poverty and pollution began to live alongside one another, as houses became overcrowded and rubbish quickly filled the streets.

By the 1850s, over 2 million people lived in London, but the city, in spite of its growing popularity and wealth, found it difficult to cope with such an influx of people. Diseases such as cholera and typhoid spread easily, and the infrastructure of the city began to flounder. Often a great stench lay over the houses, making it difficult to face going outdoors, especially in the summer months. A general lack of scientific knowledge existed, which meant many believed that the miasma of rotten, foul smelling air hanging over London's streets caused the spread of diseases.

Cholera outbreak

In 1854, London was in the middle of suffering one of its worst cholera outbreaks. Over 600 people living in Broad Street, in the district of Soho, died from the disease. However, one of the benefits arising from the tragedy was that Dr John Snow's study of the illness led him to the conclusion that germs in the water were not only the cause of cholera, but also a means of it spreading. With this knowledge, gradually, sanitation and public health began to improve not just in London, but around Great Britain.

Unfortunately, in many of the poorest areas, this did not happen quickly enough, and as a result, poverty, lack of work, and general dissatisfaction inevitably led to a rise in crime among the least well-off. Their crimes ranged from the everyday theft of basics, such as food, to the much darker crime of murder. The murder of children, even by parents, seems to have been widely reported, and it is interesting to consider whether some parents, driven to despair through lack of funds and proper housing, felt the only option open to them was to be rid of their newborn babies as quickly as possible. To a twenty-first century reader, the crime of infanticide seems too repulsive to imagine, but to a mid-nineteenth-century parent, with no money, no way of earning an income, and only the workhouse to look forward to, perhaps death seemed a better option than experiencing life in a seemingly cruel and unjust society. An article which appeared in *The London Daily News* on 3 April 1850 detailed the case of a baby killed by its father:

Assize Intelligence – Home Circuit

Thomas Denny, 32, was indicted for the wilful murder of a certain unbaptised male child, by stabbing it in the throat with an awl.

A woman, named Eliza Tarrent, was originally included in the charge, but the grand jury ignored the bill against her.

Mr Locke conducted the prosecution on behalf of the parish authorities of Ewell. The prisoner was defended by Mr Clarke.

The learned counsel for the prosecution having opened the case, the following evidence was adduced:

Anne Dunford stated that she was a widow, and resided at Ewell. On the 16th of August last, in consequence of some communication that was made to her, she went, accompanied by Sarah Trigg, and another person, to a loft over a yard belonging to a person named Moore, at Ewell. She there saw a woman named Eliza Tarrent, lying apparently in a helpless state, with a new-born babe by her side. She observed that the child bled from the nose and mouth, and none of the usual precautions in such cases had been taken with respect to it. The prisoner was also in the loft, but at witness's suggestion he went away. She remained in attendance upon Eliza Tarrent about an hour, and witness's daughter then took the child to her house. The child was carried down the ladder leading to and from the loft by one of the women, and not by the prisoner. Witness shortly afterwards washed the baby, and then observed a wound on the neck, and she also saw that it was bruised upon the body. After she had done what she considered necessary to the child she took it back to its mother, and it died about an hour afterwards. The prisoner then went away and made a coffin, and he said it must be buried. Witness told him it would be necessary to have the death registered, and he made some answer which she did not hear. Mr Lane, the surgeon, afterwards came to the loft, when she showed him the body of the infant.

Cross-examined – The prisoner fetched her to go and see Eliza Tarrent. She was lying upon straw in the loft, and the child's throat appeared to have been scratched by the litter that was lying about. She stated this at the time. The prisoner went with her to a gentleman's house in the neighbourhood to get some linen for Eliza Tarrent. She remembered saying to the prisoner that she did not think the poor thing would live, and he replied, 'it will be a happy thing for it can never go better than now, with no sins to answer for.'

James Denny, a son of the prisoner, was then placed in the witness box to be examined. He stated that he was 8 years old.

He was accordingly examined. He said – The prisoner is my father. Eliza Tarrent used to live with my father. We all lived together in the hayloft at Ewell. I recollect Eliza Tarrent having a baby; I went to my father when it happened and told him to come home directly as mother was very ill, and he did so. When we got back I saw Eliza Tarrent lying in the loft, and a baby by her. My father took up the baby in his arms; he then took up an awl – (here the poor child became much affected, and cried bitterly, and it was some time before he could proceed with his testimony; at length he went on) – my father took up the awl, and killed the baby with it; he struck it with the awl. My father then took the child to Eliza Tarrent and asked her if he should make a coffin for it. Before he said this he asked her if she would help to kill it, and gave her the awl. She did try to kill it also. My father gave her the child and the awl, and she did the same that he had done. I was very much frightened at what I saw, and ran away, and when I came back I found Eliza Tarrent in bed.

James Denny went on to tell the court that while his father had been in prison, he had been living in a workhouse. The rest of the article makes it clear that Eliza Tarrent and Thomas Denny were not married, but had been living together in the hay loft for two years. James Denny was Thomas Denny's son from a previous relationship. It is also made clear that Thomas Denny was prone to outbursts of temper and that he refused to allow Eliza to make clothes in preparation for the baby's birth. The stigma of having an illegitimate child in the nineteenth century could make life particularly difficult for a family. The fact that they were so poor they were forced to live in a hay loft compounds their problem further. Contraception was not easily available to those couples – whether married or not – who had little or no income, and perhaps the thought of one more mouth to feed proved too much for Thomas Denny. Whatever the case, it drove him to an act of unthinkable violence. The jury found him guilty within an hour and he was sentenced to death, and warned to expect no hope of a last-minute reprieve. However, in spite of this stipulation, on 24 April Thomas Denny was granted a free pardon due to a lack of evidence.

It was London, a city filled with squalor and crime, that George Eliot contemplated making her new home. It was a city which looked down upon its poor and paid homage to its rich. But it was also a city blessed with culture and the arts, a city which encouraged literary conversation, political and religious debate, the new and the modern. As a woman looking for a new start, it was a city which appeared to hold much promise.

Further tragedy

Unfortunately, the death of her father was not the only bereavement George Eliot was to suffer within a short space of time. Before the end of the 1850s, both her sister Chrissey and her brother-in-law, Dr Clarke, would be dead. Chrissey had been the only sibling to offer any support and kindness to her sister after the death of their father. Lack of funds and the burden of a large family meant that in practical terms, Chrissey was unable to do anything to help her sister, but it seems her kindness was never forgotten.

Readers have often commented on the autobiographical nature of *The Mill on the Floss,* and on the similarities between the childhood of Maggie Tulliver and George Eliot. Other similarities are also plain to see – Tom Tulliver and Isaac Evans share the same intolerance towards their sister's behaviour – and both Maggie and her creator have a much closer relationship with their father than their mother. However, there is another character in particular who, in both her relationship with her husband and in suffering the fate that befalls her, bears a striking resemblance to George Eliot's own sister, Chrissey. Mr Tulliver's sister, 'poor Gritty', in a manner similar to Chrissey Evans seems to seal her own downfall through her marriage to Moss, for as her brother declares, she 'had quite thrown herself away in marriage and had crowned her mistakes by having an eighth baby'. Indeed, before this sad occurrence, he believed her to be, 'a good looking wench', and is angry at the loan he has to make Moss, due to him being, 'a man without capital'. Even when Mr Tulliver is struggling financially and is in desperate need of money himself, he cannot bring himself to demand of Moss the capital he has loaned him. To do so would be to make his sister's whole family bankrupt and homeless. Moss's farm is described near the end of the book and the poverty of the Moss family, who live outside the boundaries of the much more genteel St Ogg's, is once again reinforced:

> She was standing on the causeway with her aunt and a group of cousins feeding the chickens, at that quiet moment in the life of the farmyard before the afternoon milking-time. The great buildings round the hollow yard were as dreary and tumbledown as ever, but over the old garden wall the straggling rose-bushes were beginning to toss their

summer weight, and the grey wood and old bricks of the house, on its higher level, had a look of sleepy age in the broad afternoon sunlight, that suited the quiescent time. Maggie, with her bonnet over her arm, was smiling down at a hatch of small fluffy chickens.

(Book Six, Chapter 11, *The Mill on the Floss*)

The faded, shabby appearance of the Moss farm reflects that of Mrs Moss herself. Once considered beautiful, she is now tired and worn both in appearance and physicality due to financial concerns and the burden of having too many children over a relatively short period of time. After her marriage to Dr Clarke, George Eliot's sister Chrissey suffered a similar fate. Driven to bankruptcy through a mixture of living beyond his means and having more children than he could afford, Dr Clarke was forced to borrow money from his father-in-law, knowing full well it was a loan he could ill-afford to pay back. He died in relative poverty in 1852. Poor Chrissey never fully regained her health. She remained fragile and frail and died just seven short years later, at only 45 years of age. She left behind six surviving children, but in actual fact had given birth to nine babies: an emotional and bodily toll that certainly had a huge effect on her mental as well as her physical well-being. But it must not be forgotten that many of the women who lived in mid-nineteenth-century Britain had pregnancy forced upon them, as there was little or no alternative offered in the form of contraception, and without doubt such knowledge would, in any case, remain hidden to genteel women of limited means. Instead, women of the middle-classes were expected to relish their role as mothers, as a large family was believed to be a sign of health and happiness within the marital home. Women like Chrissey had little choice but to fulfil their obligations as wives, however ill the resulting pregnancies might leave them. Both Chrissey Clarke and her fictional counterpart Mrs Moss were forced to pay the price for this during their lives.

George Eliot was searching for something different when she decided to move to London. Certainly, she was hoping for more than a life living in the shadow of debt. The answer was to be provided by John Chapman and the *Westminster Review*.

Chapter Seven

In which George Eliot finds work with the *Westminster Review*, meets G H Lewes, and leaves England

There was something which she now felt profoundly to be the best thing that life could give her. But – if it was to be had at all – it was not to be had without paying a heavy price for it, such as we must pay for all that is greatly good. A supreme love, a motive that gives a sublime rhythm to a woman's life, and exalts habit into partnership with the soul's highest needs, is not to be had where and how she wills: to know that high initiation, she must often tread where it is hard to tread, and feel the chill air, and watch through darkness.

(*Felix Holt: The Radical*)

Before her move to London could be seriously contemplated, George Eliot needed recommendations of places to stay from people she could trust. John Chapman, the publisher of the Strauss work she had translated, owned a property in the Strand. Number 142 was well-known to those intellectuals looking for an interesting and lively place to stay. Within its walls it housed a collection of people, many of them young and keen to become acquainted with London's reputation as a cultured city of literature and the arts. It was home to Chapman's own family as well as a succession of paying guests, and could sometimes be a little shambolic – lodgers tended to come and go – and evening debates could become unwieldy. Coupled with this was Chapman's own unhappy marriage. Mrs Susanna Chapman was older than her husband by over a decade and lacked his intellect and charm. However, after staying with the Chapman household for a few weeks, George Eliot was convinced that number

142 could become her new home. Her years spent visiting Rosehill had given her the confidence she needed to participate in academic debates. She was far less gauche than she had been, and although still conscious of her 'plainness', she realised that more importantly, she could hold her own on an intellectual level. At the same time, Chapman gave George Eliot the opportunity to write a review of Robert Mackay's *The Progress of the Intellect* which he hoped to see published in the *Westminster Review*.

The Progress of the Intellect was an ideal book for George Eliot to review. Once again, the nature of religion was being challenged, as well as the way academics tended to mythologise the nature of Christianity and its biblical interpretation. The complexities of Mackay's argument are apparent even from its opening:

> It is impossible that man in the infancy of his faculties should be intellectually or spiritually religious. Impressed with a vague idea of superior external power, he is ignorant of its extent and character. His first attempts to scan the invisible are like the efforts of the undisciplined eye to apprehend the remote. The child tries to touch the distant horizon, and the uncultivated mind hopes to obtain impressions of the Deity equally palpable to the senses. God is seen in the clouds or heard in the wind; everything uncomprehended is at once referred to supernatural agency, just as a pool of unknown depth is supposed by popular credulity to be unfathomable.
>
> (Chapter 1, Elements of the Mythical)

Yet George Eliot was able to read and respond to *The Progress of the Intellect* without being afraid to challenge Mackay on some of the arguments he made throughout his book. From her very first review, therefore, she was able to make a suitable impression not just on the readers of the *Westminster Review*, but most importantly on John Chapman himself. Even by reading just an extract from her response, the twenty-first century reader is given a tantalising glimpse into the mind and intellect of George Eliot:

> It is in his theory concerning the religious development of the Hebrews, and in his treatment of their records,

that Mr Mackay departs the most widely from prevalent opinion. The idea that many parts of the Old Testament have a mythical character, an idea which was necessary to conciliate them, as well with the philosophical Hebrewism of Philo, as with the Christian morality of Origen, and which has long been familiar to German critics, is still startling to the English theological mind. No thinker of ordinary intelligence can fail to perceive, not merely difference in degree of completeness, but contrast, between the religious conceptions which represented the deity as sanctioning or prescribing the cunning trickery of Jacob, or the savage cruelties of Joshua, and those which preside over the sublime remonstrances of the prophets; but the explanation is still sought in the theory of accommodation that is the puerile and unworthy religious conceptions invariably accompanying an absence of intellectual culture, which in other nations are referred to the general principles of human development, are, in the case of the Hebrews, supposed to have been benevolent falsities on the part of the true God, whereby he allured a barbarous race to his recognition and worship.

Such an astute academic commentary and such insightful remarks ensured George Eliot's response to Mackay's *The Progress of the Intellect* was ideal material for the *Westminster Review*.

The *Westminster Review* was founded in 1823 by Jeremy Bentham. It ran for just under 100 years and was notable for its radical views and the quality of its contributors, the most notable of whom included John Stuart Mill, Mary Shelley, Herbert Spencer and Thomas Huxley. Although the paper initially sold numbers of up to 3,000, making it appear successful, financially it was a failure and Bentham realised that he was unable to break even, let alone make a profit. By the end of the 1820s, Bentham's funding had run out and he was forced to sell the paper, along for a time with its radical ideals.

When John Chapman took over in 1851, the *Westminster Review* once again renewed its radical roots, welcoming articles that valued independence of thought and looked forward to a time of progress and modernity. The ethos of the paper, therefore, was entirely suited to George Eliot's beliefs, and her reaffirmed determination to become intellectually confident. What she might not have realised at first, however, was that the house she was about to lodge in was often in an emotionally chaotic state, due mostly to housing not just John Chapman's wife, but also his lover.

John Chapman

Born in Nottingham in 1821, it was not only his house that could accurately be described as emotionally chaotic, but also Chapman himself. From a young age he had lived away from home in his role as an apprentice watchmaker, but he seldom seemed to suffer from homesickness or any concerns about his place in the world. This may be the result of having two pieces of good fortune on his side: good looks and confidence. At the same time, his interest in various subjects encouraged him to attend lectures and meetings, and this added to his feeling of being fully equipped to meet the world head-on. He did not intend to remain a watchmaker forever. Indeed, his sights were set considerably higher and his confidence in his own abilities led to him purchasing a quantity of watches and setting sail for Australia, with the obvious intention of making his fortune. On his return home he trained for several years as a doctor, before marrying his wife Susanna, an heiress whose father had made his money in the manufacture of lace. Her family was against the marriage, suggesting perhaps that Chapman had not made his fortune in Australia, for he apparently brought very little to the relationship other than his handsome appearance. Susanna was almost fifteen years older than him and her family was concerned, no doubt, that the love of this much younger man began and ended with her fortune. Nevertheless, they were married by special licence and began their life as husband and wife in London.

John Chapman was nothing if not eager to display his many and varied talents, and so shortly after settling into married life he wrote a book. If the length of the book was considered small, its title was most certainly not: *Human Nature; A Philosophical Exposition of the Divine Institution of Reward and Punishment which obtains in the Physical, Intellectual and Moral Constitutions of Man; with an Introductory Essay. To which is Added a Series of Ethical Observations Written During the Perusal of the Reverend James Martineau's Recent Work Entitled Endeavours after the Christian Life*. In the first instance, Chapman offered his manuscript to the publisher John Green of Newgate Street. Although he was interested in the book, Green explained that he was actually selling his publishing concern. Somehow, Chapman managed to persuade his wife to allow him to use some of her inheritance to buy Green's business. Within a short while, John Chapman was a publisher as well as a prospective author. Most importantly, some might say, he was also a father to a baby daughter. Beatrice was born at the end of 1844, pre-empting a move to a more suitable house in Upper Clapton Common. Within two years, which included the birth of a son, Ernest, and the beginning of Chapman's pre-eminence on the literary scene as the host of notable talks and debates, the family had moved once again to 142 the Strand, and it was here that George Eliot became properly acquainted with the Chapmans. It was also the house on the Strand which first introduced Chapman's lodger to his rather colourful life and his belief that a wife was never enough to fulfil all of his needs. It was this conviction which led to the emotional upheaval in John Chapman's life, as well as in the lives of those closely associated with him.

When George Eliot arrived at 142 the Strand, she had no intention of becoming involved with John Chapman in any other way than as a colleague and friend. Indeed, she was determined to see him mostly as a potential employer, someone who could offer her work at the *Westminster Review* and who could hopefully introduce her to some interesting and worthwhile people. At the same time, it did not take long for her to realise that Chapman already had a mistress living under his roof. Elisabeth Tilley, nursemaid and nanny to Beatrice and Ernest, was fulfilling any need that his wife Susanna could not, meaning that Chapman was dealing with the dangerous prospect of living with his wife and his mistress under one roof. However, Chapman managed somehow to exert his charm over George Eliot and in due course, he found himself living with not just one mistress under the same roof as his wife, but two. Strangely, while most men would try to avoid such a possible calamity, John Chapman seemed to thrive on the occurrence of potential drama between the three women and looked forward to the emotional chaos that might ensue should their jealousy of each other threaten to spill over into something more violent.

It was not long before Susanna, who was painfully conscious of Elisabeth's role in her husband's life, was made aware that their new lodger was also a contender for his time and attention. Having a husband with one mistress was just about bearable, but to have a husband with two mistresses under their roof was beyond reproach. A strange turn of events saw Elisabeth and Susanna join forces against the latest interloper and the atmosphere at 142 the Strand became unbearable. At the same time, John Chapman did the unthinkable and told George Eliot that while he admired her intellect greatly, he loved his wife and Elisabeth, albeit in different ways. Not for the first time, she found herself journeying back to Coventry ready for a stay in Rosehill, her new start apparently over before it was begun. However, this time, something different occurred which changed the prospective writer's fortunes. Having recently taken over the *Westminster Review*, John Chapman was eager to find a suitable associate editor, someone with the intellect and literary ability to lead the magazine successfully through its next revival. Chapman made the trip to Coventry and eventually persuaded George Eliot to take up the post he offered her, although the conditions were not entirely favourable. He made it quite clear that he was not willing to give up his relationship with Elisabeth Tilley. Indeed, he made it obvious that nothing between them could happen which might jeopardise his relationship with Miss Tilley. He also made it clear that as an associate editor, she would be anonymous. She was entering the world of men and to the outside world at least, the pretence that she was a man had to be maintained. In other words, she would remain anonymous and the reading public would remain unaware of the good work she completed. It was six years before she would publish *The Sad Fortunes of Amos Barton* and adopt the name George Eliot. Until then, anonymity was the only way she could expect to be paid for her work without causing a scandal.

Jane Eyre

It must have been frustrating for women like George Eliot – intelligent, articulate and academically-minded – to have to remain in the shadows, unable to take praise for the hard work they completed and unable to openly acknowledge the commendations and compliments that rightfully belonged to them. Perhaps more irritating was the fact that they were denied the right to at least challenge those reviews which were less than favourable, or reviewers who had missed the point of their work completely. When Charlotte Brontë's *Jane Eyre* was published by Smith, Elder and Co. in 1847, it was done so under the pseudonym of Currer Bell, the publisher perhaps afraid that revealing the true gender of the author would incite scandal – that is if anyone bothered to purchase

a book written by a woman in the first place. Although many of the
initial reviews of *Jane Eyre* were negative, focusing as they did on what
Elizabeth Rigby termed in her review its 'horrid taste', others praised the
novel for its many fundamental differences to other pieces of literature
that were being written at the time. Interestingly, one such reviewer was
George Henry Lewes, soon to play an important role in George Eliot's
life. He earned some dissatisfaction from Brontë for suggesting in his
mostly positive review that the author of *Jane Eyre* must surely be a
woman. She felt that this took away interest from her novel and instead
caused the public to reflect much more on the author. This aside, Lewes's
comments allow twenty-first-century readers to understand his instincts,
his modern thinking in accepting a woman could be intelligent enough
to write such a novel, and to appreciate why he was to become the perfect
partner for George Eliot:

> This indeed is a book after our own heart; and, if its merits
> have not forced it into notice by the time this paper comes
> before our readers, let us, in all earnestness, bid them lose
> not a day in sending for it. The writer is evidently a woman,
> and, unless we are deceived, new to the world of literature.
> But, man or woman, young or old, be that as it may, no such
> book has gladdened our eyes for a long while. Almost all
> that we require in a novelist she has: perception of character,
> and power of delineating it; picturesqueness, passion; and
> knowledge of life. The story is not only of singular interest,
> naturally evolved, unflagging to the last, but it fastens itself
> upon your attention, and will not leave you. The book closed,
> the enchantment continues. With the disentanglement
> of the plot, and the final release of the heroine from her
> difficulties, your interest does not cease. You go back again
> in memory to the various scenes in which she has figured;
> you linger on the way and muse upon the several incidents
> in the life which has just been unrolled before you, affected
> by them as if they were the austere instructions drawn from
> a sorrowing existence, and not merely the cunning devices
> of an author's craft. Reality – deep, significant reality – is
> the great characteristic of the book. It is an autobiography –
> not perhaps in the native facts and circumstances, but in the
> actual suffering and experience. The form may be changed,

and here and there some incidents invented; but the spirit remains as it was. The machinery of the story may have been borrowed, but by means of this machinery the authoress is unquestionably setting forth her own experience. This gives the book its charm; it is soul speaking to soul; it is an utterance from the depths of a struggling, suffering, much-enduring spirit: suspiria de profundis.

(*Fraser's* Magazine, 1847)

There are several things worthy of note in this extract from Lewes's review. The first is his insistence that the author of *Jane Eyre* is female. He refers to her as an authoress and seems determined that only a woman could have written such a novel. That is not to say, however, that he denigrates its style and content. Unlike other critics of nineteenth-century female writers, he praises it highly and suggests the public buy a copy as soon as they can. Other contemporary reviewers concerned themselves with *Jane Eyre*'s perceived lack of morality or Christian guidance, but Lewes focuses instead on the biographical nature of Brontë's novel and on his belief that the author must have lived through similar experiences to those of the protagonist. This is an integral part of *Jane Eyre* and one that many reviewers, overly keen on dismissing the novel as the work of a Chartist and a rebel, missed commenting upon. Perhaps most important of all is Lewes's focus on the realism of *Jane Eyre*. Many novels until this time had been sensationalist, focusing instead on moments of high drama: secrets from the past, the abduction of virtuous young women, ghosts, a castle setting, and complex and contrived plots. In her novel, Brontë had been careful to avoid such distractions by focusing on the emotional development of the protagonist and allowing the reader to glimpse her intimate thoughts through the first-person narration. Lewes's championing of Brontë's use of realism foreshadows his later relationship with George Eliot when he guides her, convincing her she has the talent to write, and suggesting she use her own memories as a starting point.

However, when George Eliot began her role at the *Westminster Review*, her relationship with Lewes was still some way in the future. For the time being, she once again had to become used to being anonymous, and to putting in many hours' work for little, if any, public recognition. This must have been even more frustrating as, although she was ostensibly the journal's associate editor, she was in effect, its editor. When he first suggested to her that she would be suitable for the role, John Chapman was fully aware that he had numerous other commitments that would mean leaving the bulk of the editorial work to his associate editor. He also knew that George Eliot was far more suited to the role than he was. His thoughts were justified when she did her best to steer the finances of the *Westminster Review* in the right direction, even when Chapman's financial mismanagement seemed to be taking the journal's bank balance in another way entirely. George Eliot's intellect, along with her sound reasoning, can be glimpsed fully in the editors' introduction to the prospectus of the *Westminster Review*, written shortly after she was appointed as associate editor:

> The Newly-appointed editors will endeavour to confirm and extend the influence of the Review as an instrument for the development and guidance of earnest thought on Politics, social philosophy, Religion, and General Literature; and to this end they will seek to render it the organ of the most able and independent minds of the day...
>
> In the department of General Literature the criticism will be animated by desire to elevate the standard of the public taste, in relation both to artistic perfection and moral purity; larger space will be afforded for articles intrinsically valuable by the omission of those minor and miscellaneous notices which are necessarily forestalled by newspapers and magazines, and equivalent information will be given in a series of Historical and Critical Sketches of Contemporary literature, comprehending a notice of the most remarkable books, both English and foreign, that may appear during each successive quarter.

Within a decade, George Eliot herself would be contributing to this canon of 'most remarkable books', but in the meantime, she had to satisfy herself with reviewing and commenting on those titles published by other writers. In one of her reviews, published in 1855, it is interesting to note George Eliot mourning the lack of new books appearing. She wrote:

> The dearth of new books just now gives us time to recur to less recent ones which we have hitherto noticed but slightly;

and among these we choose the late edition of Margaret Fuller's *Woman in the Nineteenth Century*, because we think it has been unduly thrust into the background by less comprehensive and candid productions on the same subject. Notwithstanding certain defects of taste and a sort of vague spiritualism and grandiloquence which belongs to all but the very best American writers, the book is a valuable one: it has the enthusiasm of a noble and sympathetic nature, with the moderation and breadth and large allowance of a vigorous and cultivated understanding. There is no exaggeration of woman's moral excellence or intellectual capabilities; no injudicious insistence on her fitness for this or that function hitherto engrossed by men; but a calm plea for the removal of unjust laws and artificial restrictions, so that the possibilities of her nature may have room for full development.

Her review also gives us a glimpse into her thoughts on the problems facing women living in the middle of the nineteenth century. She is obviously concerned about the high moral standards women are generally expected to maintain and wary about the restrictions that are continually forced upon them. Later, she was able to explore these issues further in her own literature.

Herbert Spencer

While beginning to experience success, albeit mainly anonymously during her time working at the *Westminster Review*, George Eliot was without the attention and love that she so often craved. A friendship she maintained with Herbert Spencer, the philosopher and anthropologist, remained a friendship, in spite of any more romantic feelings she may have developed for him. On the surface at least, they seemed an ideally suited couple. Both were intelligent and academic, both enjoyed stimulating company, but whereas George Eliot was ready for friendship to turn into romantic love, Herbert Spencer was not.

Born the son of a schoolteacher in 1820s Derby, Spencer's childhood was blighted by parental concerns for his health. Out of the five children his mother gave birth to, Herbert Spencer was the only one to survive beyond the age of 2, so it is perhaps little wonder that his parents worried for the state of his physical health. In order to protect him, the young Spencer was not educated to the standard of other children of a similar age in case the strain of learning caused him to be ill. He received no formal schooling until he was 7, firstly at a school run by Mr Mather, and secondly at a school run by his Uncle William. The problem for anyone trying to teach Spencer was that he had received very little discipline from his parents and tended to be something of a rebel.

Herbert Spencer was much more of an independent learner, preferring to discover information for himself through reading books and attending lectures on topics that interested *him*. What he did not appreciate was being forced to study subjects that other people had decided would be of use. When he was 16, his formal education was over and within a year he was working for the London and Birmingham Railway. He took his job extremely seriously, especially for someone who had once been so rebellious. He began to study subjects such as mathematics, believing they could assist him in his role and before long he was proved right and had almost 100 men working under him. Promotions led to Spencer moving around the country, before finally his unruly nature began to rear its head. He took an interest in politics, was pleased when he was sacked from the railway company, and in 1843, moved to London to work for a political newspaper. Economic instability at a variety of newspapers forced him to move several more times, and he even took jobs at different railways before the lure of London, with its intellectual and cultural hubs, once again drew his attention. It was while mingling with the London literati that he met John Chapman and through Chapman, George Eliot.

Their cerebral interests drew them into a close friendship, but as had happened several times before in her life, George Eliot began to think of the relationship in more romantic terms than the other person involved ever would. Despite spending much of 1852 together, Spencer appeared to never once consider her anything more than just a good friend. During the summer months of 1852, George Eliot spent time holidaying in Broadstairs, Kent. She was visited several times by Spencer, and this only made her fall further in love with him. The result was a letter in which she hoped that her feelings, although unrequited, would not lead to a loss of friendship between them:

> I know this letter will make you very angry with me, but wait a little and don't say anything to me while you are angry. I promise not to sin anymore in the same way.
>
> My ill health is caused by the hopeless wretchedness which weighs upon me. I do not say this to pain you, but because it is the simple truth which you must know in order to understand why I am obliged to seek relief.
>
> I want to know if you can assure me that you will not forsake me, that you will always be with me as much as you can and share your thoughts and feelings with me. If you become attached to someone else, then I must die, but until then I could gather courage to work and make life valuable, if only I had you near me. I do not ask you to sacrifice anything – I would be very good and cheerful and never annoy you. But I find it impossible to contemplate life under any other conditions. If I had your assurance, I could trust that and live upon it. I have struggled – indeed I have – to renounce everything and be entirely unselfish, but I find myself utterly unequal to it. Those who have known me best have always said that if ever I loved any one thoroughly my whole life must turn upon that feeling, and I found they said truly. You curse the destiny which has made the feeling concentrate itself on you – but if you will only have patience with me you shall not curse it long. You will find that I can be satisfied with very little, if I am delivered from the dread of losing it.
>
> I suppose no woman ever before wrote such a letter as this – but I am not ashamed of it, for I am conscious that in the light of reason and true refinement I am worthy of your respect and tenderness whatever gross men or vulgar-minded women might think of me.
>
> (George Eliot Letters, Volume 8)

If only George Eliot had known then what readers know now: that Herbert Spencer never married. Indeed, he died a bachelor at the age of 83.

Had she been fortunate enough to have access to this knowledge, she need never have spent time worrying that she might be ousted from Spencer's life by someone whom he found more interesting, and more attractive. In truth, Herbert Spencer enjoyed George Eliot's companionship. She was amusing, academic and was an easy match for his intelligence. Someone with these attributes was not always easy to find, and so giving up her friendship was not on Spencer's agenda, even if he did not plan on offering a proposal of marriage. George Eliot's letter reveals her quiet dignity, her determination and inner strength, all laudable qualities. But it is also an important letter for another reason. It was to be the last letter she would need to write where she asked, even begged, another human for their affection.

George Henry Lewes

As soon as it became clear Spencer was unable to offer anything other than friendship, George Eliot refused to relinquish her self-respect. Indeed, she began to spend more time with a friend of Spencer's and someone he himself had introduced her to. George Henry Lewes had once been described, somewhat unfairly, as the 'ugliest man in London'. Yet portraits and photographs of Lewes present a man of gentle, if serious expression, with a wide face, a somewhat narrow chin, facial hair worn very much as the period dictated and pleasantly expressive eyes.

He had first met George Eliot very briefly in 1851, in a bookshop in London's Burlington Arcade. A friend of Herbert Spencer, Lewes was somewhat taken by George Eliot, and the meeting in Burlington's seems to have left a greater impression on Lewes than it did on her. This is perhaps hardly surprising as she was still in the throes of her burgeoning love for Spencer, and was hardly likely to be swept off her feet by one of his friends. However, Lewes began to pay visits to her office at the *Westminster Review*, even when not accompanying Herbert Spencer, and when she realised Spencer was not in any way forming a romantic attachment to her, she began to relax a little in Lewes's company. She undoubtedly found him amusing; indeed, he could be jovial and funny, and their joint interests in culture, politics and literature meant that there was always something interesting for them to talk about. Only one thing appeared to stand in the way of their warm friendship becoming something more, and for once it was not over-clinginess or possessiveness on George Eliot's part. Lewes was already married and mid-nineteenth century society was in no way ready to contemplate an open relationship between a spinster in her thirties and a married man.

Lewes's history

George Henry Lewes was born in London in 1817. He lived with his mother and stepfather, his father having died when Lewes was very young. Like Herbert Spencer, Lewes's education was somewhat erratic, and he spent much of his childhood teaching himself. Self-education was an important part of life for many in the nineteenth century and Herbert Spencer, George Henry Lewes and George Eliot were not alone in their constant desire to acquire more knowledge. Charles Dickens, Charlotte, Emily and Anne Brontë all benefited from using magazines and journals, as well as books and public talks, to expand their knowledge or to fill in any gaps left by the somewhat patchy formal education they had received. In the case of the Brontë sisters, the poor conditions they were subjected to at Cowan Bridge School are believed to have inspired Charlotte Brontë in her creation of Lowood Institution, which was attended by the eponymous Jane Eyre, and was the source of much of her misery in her formative years. Indeed, the lack of facilities and inadequate conditions at Cowan Bridge led to the deaths of both of the Brontës' elder sisters. Maria and Elizabeth Brontë were withdrawn from Cowan Bridge in 1824, only to die from tuberculosis at home shortly afterwards. In Chapter Seven of *Jane Eyre*, Charlotte Brontë writes a clear account of the harsh conditions suffered by the pupils at Lowood and, given the illnesses suffered by her sisters, it seems highly likely that she is writing from experience:

> My first quarter at Lowood seemed an age; and not the golden age either; it comprised an irksome struggle with difficulties in habituating myself to new rules and unwonted tasks. The fear of failure in these points harassed me worse than the physical hardships of my lot; though these were no trifles.
> During January, February and part of March, the deep snows, and after their melting, the almost impassable roads,

prevented our stirring beyond the garden walls, except to go to church; but within these limits we had to pass an hour every day in the open air. Our clothing was insufficient to protect us from the severe cold: we had no boots, the snow got into our shoes and melted there; our ungloved hands became numbed and covered with chilblains, as were our feet; I remember well the distracting irritation I endured from this cause, every evening when my feet inflamed; and the torture of thrusting the swelled, raw and stiff toes into my shoes in the morning. Then, the scanty supply of food was distressing: with the keen appetites of growing children, we had scarcely sufficient to keep alive a delicate invalid.

Earlier, Brontë describes just how awful the little amount of food they were served actually tasted:

Ravenous, and now very faint, I devoured a spoonful or two of my portion without thinking of its taste; but the first edge of hunger blunted, I perceived I got in hand a nauseous mess: burnt porridge is almost as bad as rotten potatoes; famine itself soon sickens over it. The spoons were moved slowly: I saw each girl taste her food and try to swallow it; but in most cases the effort was soon relinquished. Breakfast was over, and none had breakfasted.

(Chapter Five, *Jane Eyre*)

It is little wonder, therefore, that the Brontë sisters seemed to fare better when they were either educated at home or left to their own devices. Between them and their brother Branwell, they created the imaginary worlds that helped to hone the writing skills that served them so well in later life.

In the case of Charles Dickens, family poverty and debt meant that instead of being educated, he was sent to work in a blacking factory, and from a young age was forced to contribute to the family finances. Although the 1833 Factory Act was meant to ensure that all employers provided workers under 13 with some form of part-time education, the legislation was easy to ignore as no checks were put in place to ascertain if this was being carried out. 1870 saw the introduction of local school boards, responsible for levying rates and using the money raised to build schools to provide education for children up to the age of 10. It was not until 1880, however, that education for all children until the age of 13 became compulsory.

George Eliot had been more fortunate than many in the formal education she had received, particularly for a female, but she still felt she had much to learn, and as a result she thrived on finding ways to develop her knowledge, and widen her academic reading. Similarly, in spite of his less-than-satisfactory formal education, the same spark that ignited his future partner's desire to learn also fanned a similar flame in George Henry Lewes. He taught himself a variety of languages, including Greek and German, and developed an interest in anatomy. He sampled a number of careers, including working for a leather merchant, but there is little doubt that he found his out-of-work activities of much more interest. In his spare time Lewes enjoyed discussing philosophy and religion, passions which became life-long pursuits. Through his career as a journalist, which he began after spending two years in Germany teaching English, he met such interesting and influential people as Thomas Carlyle and William Makepeace Thackeray, and enjoyed a degree of success, having his articles accepted for publication in a variety of journals.

His romantic life also appeared to be just as successful and to many, Lewes seemed to be leading something of a charmed life. He had met Agnes, the daughter of Swynfen Jervis, the Liberal MP for Bridport, when employed as a tutor for the Jervis family. Agnes was a noted beauty, with long blonde hair, blue eyes and a porcelain-pale complexion. When the couple were married in February 1841, Lewes was considered to be an extremely fortunate man.

Luckily for Lewes, his marriage was also a meeting of minds. Agnes was a capable, educated woman who was able to make money through translating articles into French and Spanish. She was intelligent enough to engage Lewes in conversation and in the year following their marriage, the couple became parents to their firstborn, a son named Charlie. He was followed in 1844 by their second son, Thornton, and in 1846 by a third son, Herbert. Sadly, a fourth son, St Vincent Arthy, born in 1848, did not survive infancy. In these intervening years, Lewes was doing more than just fathering children. He was also writing novels, as well as articles for journals and magazines. Novel-writing proved not to be one of his most successful ventures, and Lewes fared better when it came to writing about philosophy. Despite not being academically trained, his interest in the subject meant that he was able to write with passion and vigour. Indeed, so much did he have to say that his *History of Philosophy from Thales to Comte* was spread over four volumes, and although he angered some academics for writing on a subject for which he had not been university-tutored, others believed his books to be extremely interesting. Neither was his talent at this time limited to musing upon, and writing about, philosophy. He also enjoyed a stage career, publishing a book and writing articles about acting and performing alongside Charles Dickens in his friend's amateur company.

Lewes's marriage to Agnes

Lewes's research activities often took him away from home, but even through times of separation, his marriage to Agnes, on the surface at least, appeared to be a happy one. As a couple their beliefs were similar to those of Cara and Charles Bray, and just like George Eliot's friends, they too were liberally-minded free-thinkers. Unlike many people living in mid-nineteenth-century Britain, they were adamant that living an unconventional life was absolutely nothing to be ashamed of. Whereas many new brides about to embark on married life were encouraged to read magazines and books in order to accomplish the role of the perfect wife, mother and hostess, Agnes was much too free-spirited to worry about such conventional thinking. It is difficult to imagine her spending time concerning herself with thoughts of how to feed her husband when there was literature to read and conversations to be had. One of the most popular books for eager and enthusiastic housewives to consume was *Mrs Beeton's Book of Household Management*. Published in 1861, Mrs Beeton's book contained a wealth of information on how best to handle servants and footmen, especially the truculent or untidy ones; the most effective way to perform the duties of a sick-nurse; and how to cope most patiently with the demands of a growing family. In Chapter One, Isabella Beeton had the following advice to impart to her readers about the expected etiquette required of every self-respecting mistress of the house:

> The choice of acquaintances is very important to the happiness of a mistress and her family. A gossiping acquaintance, who indulges in the scandal and ridicule

of the neighbours, should be avoided as a pestilence...
Friendships should not be hastily formed, nor the heart
given, at once, to every new-comer... Hospitality is a most
excellent virtue; but care must be taken that the love of
company, for its own sake, does not become a prevailing
passion: for then the habit is no longer hospitality but
dissipation... With respect to the continuance of friendships,
however, it may be found necessary, in some cases, for a
mistress to relinquish, on assuming the responsibility of a
household, many of those commenced in the earlier part of
her life. This will be the more requisite, if the number still
retained be quite equal to her means and opportunities.

In conversation, trifling occurrences, such as small
disappointments, petty annoyances, and other every-day
incidents, should never be mentioned to your friends... If
the mistress be a wife, never let an account of her husband's
failings pass her lips... Good temper should be cultivated by
every mistress... Every head of a household should strive
to be cheerful and should never fail to show a deep interest
in all that appertains to the well-being of those who claim
protection of her roof... her visitors are also pleased by it
and their happiness increased.

Earlier in the chapter, Mrs Beeton comments that:

She who makes her husband happy and her children happy,
who reclaims the one from vice and trains the other up to
virtue, is a much greater character than ladies described in
novels.

Given the freedom that both Agnès and Lewes enjoyed while married,
it is difficult to see how Agnes might abide by Isabella Beeton's advice
to a wife that she should not complain about her husband's 'failings' to
her friends. Indeed, it is interesting to consider how some of Agnes's
acquaintances might have reacted had they known the truth about
the Leweses' marriage. Similarly, neither Agnes nor Lewes might
be considered by the standards of the time in any position to raise
each other up from 'vice' when we consider that they had each given
their blessing for the other to have an affair. Agnes's father, the MP

Swynfen Jervis, was renowned for his liberal thinking. His daughter had grown up in a family of unorthodox thinkers and so there was little chance of Agnes changing when she grew into adulthood. As a couple, Lewes and Agnes believed that their marriage vows could be stretched enough to allow for some extra-marital liaisons, without these destroying the fundamentals of their life together. Neither one believed that monogamy could be naturally sustained for a lifetime, and as a result each one gave the other the freedom to indulge in an affair, should the opportunity arise. It might have come as little shock to Lewes, therefore, to discover that while he was on one of his many research trips, his wife had begun an affair with a man called Thornton Leigh Hunt. Given that while he was away from home Lewes often indulged in the odd liaison, he was willing to sanction Agnes's affair with Hunt, who was one of his own close associates. Not only had Hunt been a guest at the couple's wedding, but he and Lewes were hoping to launch a weekly magazine called the *Leader*. While apparently happy to give Agnes permission to have an affair with Hunt, Lewes's main caveat was that no babies should be born as a result of their relationship. It therefore came as something of a shock for Lewes, when he discovered that the baby Agnes had given birth to in the spring of 1850 was not in fact his, but was instead the son of Thornton Leigh Hunt. Other men, particularly those who had been brought up to acknowledge the views of such a patriarchal society, might have chosen to throw Agnes and her newborn out on the street, regardless of whether or not her lover would take pity on her. Indeed, in Hunt's case, he was unlikely to welcome his mistress into his own home, not because of a lack of care, but because of his own personal family life. To add even more drama and confusion to the situation, Thornton Leigh Hunt was already married to Katherine Gliddon, and had been since 1834.

Marriage laws

Lewes was nothing if not a man of integrity, and despite his earlier warning that Agnes should take care not to fall pregnant, he realised that by sanctioning the affair this was a risk not just undertaken by his wife and Hunt, but also by himself. Unwilling to allow Agnes's baby to be illegitimate in an era where such a label was viewed as a social crime, Lewes decided to accept the baby boy as his own and registered him as such. Little did he realise that in so doing, he was destroying his own future happiness and that of the woman with whom he would spend the rest of his life. By putting his name on the birth certificate, he was admitting that he was complicit in Agnes's adultery, and would therefore be unable to divorce his wife on these grounds should he ever wish to do so. By the stroke of a pen, he had unwittingly ostracised George Eliot to the margins of polite society on the basis of their inability to marry, and by the apparent lack of shame she would later be seen to display when living with a married man.

However, while in the middle of such tumult, Lewes had no idea that he was already beginning to shape his future. What he did begin to fully comprehend was the growing divide between agreeing to extra-marital affairs in conversation, and the actual reality of having a wife who had fallen in love with someone else. Agnes may have begun her affair with Hunt out of boredom, or because of a desire to rebel and to flout the rules that so stringently made up the essential fabric of Victorian society, but what neither Agnes nor her husband had predicted was Agnes's feelings for Hunt burgeoning into love.

Children

What undoubtedly made Agnes and Lewes's predicament worse were her further pregnancies. Lewes had been accepting of her first baby with Hunt to the point where he gave him his own name, and brought him up as his own. However, in the autumn of 1851, Agnes gave birth to their second child, a girl, who was named after her mother. In essence, the birth of Rose Agnes brought an end to the Leweses' marriage, leaving Agnes free to give birth to two more of Hunt's children, girls they named Ethel Isabella and Mildred Jane. After the birth of Rose Agnes, Lewes and Agnes stopped living under the same roof, although Lewes was willing to support Agnes financially and remained cordial towards her. Hunt, however, escaped with his marital status intact and he and his wife Katherine had a total of ten children, two of them being born only weeks apart from two of Hunt's children by Agnes.

In spite of the legal documentation still being intact, Agnes and Lewes both knew that their marriage was now a mere formality.

In Lewes's mind, it was over and he felt free to not only indulge in an affair, but to actually form a lasting and meaningful connection with a woman he could love entirely. Although he and Agnes had certainly been in love when they married, their desire to live freely had not entirely gone to plan, leaving Lewes in particular with no option but to physically remove himself from his wife's presence. Without her by his side, he now felt able to emotionally detach himself and find love where it would be equally reciprocated.

Since first meeting George Eliot in the Burlington Arcade in 1851, and through engaging her in conversation at 142 the Strand regarding the *Westminster Review*, Lewes had been more and more drawn to this woman who could tantalise him through her intellectual charms. But it was not just her talents as a conversationalist that drew Lewes to George Eliot. She was also a skilled listener, engaging animatedly whenever he talked, responding eagerly and with interest to his anecdotes and political or literary commentary. The two of them met, conversed and delighted in each other's company, each growing steadily more attracted to the other. In a letter to Cara Bray, written on 16 April 1853, George Eliot wrote the following about her time spent with Lewes:

> I am taking doses of agreeable follies, as you recommend. Last night I went to the French Theatre and tonight I am going to the opera to hear 'William Tell'. People are very good to me. Mr Lewes, especially, is kind and attentive, and has quite won my regard, after having a good deal of my vituperation. Like a few other people in the world, he is much better than he seems. A man of heart and conscience, wearing a mask of flippancy.

However, in the background, there was always the shadow of Agnes and Lewes's marriage. This was, after all, mid-nineteenth-century Britain, and the idea of the 'fallen woman' was as real and possible a fate as that of being the much-worshipped 'angel in the house'. Lewes was still a married man, and if George Eliot lived openly with him, she would be a social pariah, destined to live on the fringes of society for the rest of her life, ignored by all and with every opportunity closed to her.

Fallen women

The Victorians believed fallen women had lost their innocence in much the same way as Eve had done in the Garden of Eden. Through listening to Satan and in giving in to her temptation for the forbidden fruit, Eve essentially ensured that all women were destined to be seen as weak and malleable, easily manipulated by their less-than-finer feelings. Nineteenth-century society believed it was up to women to prove they were different, and to show patriarchal leaders that they were strong, virtuous and honest. Sex was for the domestic sphere only, and not necessarily something for females to enjoy. A woman was either a virgin waiting to be married, or a spinster destined never to enjoy the delights of marriage. Beyond this there was no other label or social sphere in existence to cater for another way of life other than that of being a prostitute or a mistress, in other words: a fallen woman.

The poet Christina Rossetti was particularly influenced by the idea of the fallen woman in her literary works. Published in 1859, the poem *Cousin Kate* tells of an innocent young maiden who is taken advantage of by a rich young lord. When he tires of her, she is abandoned, marginalised by society and forced to bring up their child alone. Although he marries another humble village maiden, they seem to be unable to have children, and the poem's narrator takes comfort from her son. Throughout the poem it becomes obvious that Rossetti is particularly interested in highlighting the double standards that supported much of Victorian society's beliefs and conventions. The village maiden is shamed for her relationship with the lord, even though she loves him:

> He wore me like a silken knot,
> He changed me like a glove;
> So now I moan, an unclean thing,
> Who might have been a dove.

The clothing imagery is indicative of how quickly the lord is able to swap the maiden for someone else. She is disposable, and her status as a girl from the working classes means he is able to disregard the impact his attitude towards her will have on her life. However, as a man, and particularly one from the upper classes, the lord is free to continue with his life and remain socially unscathed. It was believed at the time that men were less able to control their sexual impulses, and this was seen as understandable given the physical make-up of males. Women, however, were expected to keep themselves morally superior, and if they failed, many in society were only too willing to punish and marginalise them.

It was a situation which even Charles Dickens took issue with, displaying concern and sympathy for those women who found themselves discarded by society, either because poverty forced them into prostitution, or because they had been abandoned by errant husbands or by men who had promised marriage. Victorian society seemed unable to countenance women being forced into prostitution due to poverty, preferring to believe that such women were fallen, and made their living through sexual encounters simply because they enjoyed it. In 1847, with the financial support of Angela Burdett-Coutts, Dickens established Urania Cottage and populated it with women who had either fallen on hard times, been abandoned or were forced into prostitution. His aim was to educate, train and prepare them for life in domestic service in one of Great Britain's colonies, such as Australia or Canada.

David Copperfield

In 1850, Charles Dickens published *David Copperfield*, which tells the story of a middle-class boy's journey into adulthood and the lessons he learns upon the way. One of the most interesting characters in the novel is his childhood friend, Emily, who, in spite of being betrothed to the hard-working Ham, runs away with the wealthy but selfish James Steerforth, a friend of David's who has blinded him to his cruel streak. The reaction of Emily's family to the news of her departure allows us to see how strongly loved ones responded to such news. Not only has Emily broken the heart of her fiancé Ham, but he, along with the rest of her family, realise that Emily's life is going to be forever tarnished with the brush of immorality. Unless Steerforth marries her, and they are experienced enough to know this very rarely happens in such situations, Emily will be forever castigated as a fallen woman:

'Mas'r Davy!' – Oh, for his broken heart, how dreadfully he wept!

I was paralysed by the sight of such grief. I don't know what I thought, or what I dreaded. I could only look at him.

'Ham! Poor good fellow! For Heaven's sake tell what's the matter!'

'My love, Mas'r Davy – the pride and hope of my art – her that I'd have died for, and would die for now – she's gone!'

'Gone?'

'Em'ly's run away! Oh, Mas'r Davy, think how she's run away, when I pray my good and gracious God to kill her (her that is so dear above all things) sooner than let her come to ruin and disgrace!'

The face that he turned up to the troubled sky, the quivering of his clasped hands, the agony of his figure remain associated with that lonely waste, in my remembrance, to this hour. It is always night there, and he is the only object in the scene.

'You're a scholar,' he said, hurriedly, 'and know what's right and best. What am I to say in-doors? How am I ever to break it to him, Mas'r Davy?'

I saw the door move, and instinctively tried to hold the latch on the outside, to gain a moment's time. It was too late. Mr Peggotty thrust forth his face; and never could I forget the change that came upon it when he saw us, if I were to live five hundred years.

I remember a great wail and cry, and the women hanging about him, and we all standing in the room; I with a paper in my hand, which Ham had given me; Mr Peggotty, with his vest torn open, his hair wild, his face and lips quite white, and blood trickling down his bosom (it had sprung from his mouth, I think), looking fixedly at me.

(Chapter XXXI, *David Copperfield*)

Such is the family's grief, and such is Ham's understanding of what happens to women whose purity and innocence have been compromised, he would rather Emily die than face recriminations from a hard and overly-judgemental society.

George Eliot also introduced the idea of the fallen woman into her work with the character of Hetty Sorrel, who appears in her novel *Adam Bede*. Although Hetty has few good qualities, it is impossible to blame her completely for her actions. She is described as having, 'a false air of innocence', which is compared to:

> the innocence of a young star-browed calf, for example, that, being inclined for a promenade out of bounds, leads you a severe steeple-chase over hedge and ditch, and only comes to a stand in the middle of a bog.

The reader is also told that she has 'quite a self-possessed, coquettish air, slily conscious that no turn of the head was lost'. However, we are further reminded that she is motherless and as a result is being brought up by her aunt, who tries her best to steer Hetty on the road towards goodness, but she is only 17 and therefore easily taken advantage of. Hetty is aware of her own sexuality but her youth makes her unsure of how best to use it wisely, ensuring she is easy prey for the more mature and experienced Captain Donnithorne. Although her role as the fallen woman is offset by the virtuous Dinah Morris, George Eliot allows us to feel some sympathy for Hetty in spite of the fact that she commits infanticide by abandoning her newly-born, illegitimate baby. Hetty has transgressed, but she has been sinned against, and had she not been abandoned by the man who took advantage of her, her life would no doubt have turned out differently.

It is little wonder, therefore, that both George Eliot and George Henry Lewes realised they would have to be cautious before embarking openly on a relationship that led to them living together. Most importantly, they both realised that the negative impact on George Eliot's reputation would be far greater than that on Lewes. One of the biggest problems they faced was that they were so well-known, certainly in the capital, that even moving to a different part of the city was out of the question. If they moved to one of London's outer boroughs they still risked being recognised, word of their whereabouts and their unconventional living arrangements would undoubtedly spread and they could not allow such gossip to trail in their wake. The only idea that seemed at all possible was a temporary move abroad, and in a gesture which not only highlighted their modern approach to life, but which would simultaneously have further scandalised nineteenth-century society, they decided upon a trial' time of living together, perhaps to ensure they really were destined to be a couple. After all, it would be a shame to risk damaging their reputations only to discover that they very quickly grew tired of each other's company. The European destination they chose was Germany. Lewes was preparing to write a biography about Goethe, and George Eliot had an understanding of the language having already completed several pieces of important translation work. However, even their preparations for leaving Britain were fraught with difficulty, making it seem as if they might never be together.

Chapter Eight

In which George Eliot lives, loves and thrives while in exile

It is a wonderful subduer, this need of love – this
hunger of the heart – as peremptory as that other
hunger by which Nature forces us to submit to the yoke,
and change the face of the world.

(*The Mill on the Floss*)

Deciding to move for a period of time to another country with a partner would be considered a risk by many people in any era. To do so with a man who was still married to someone else, and therefore still legally and economically responsible for them and their children, at a time when as a woman you could be cast aside for such an action, took a great deal of courage and conviction. It comes as no surprise, therefore, to discover that both George Eliot and Lewes became unwell in the months preceding their departure for Germany. In the spring of 1854, Lewes developed neurological problems – tinnitus, constant headaches and a general feeling of ill health which he was unused to – being a man who usually wore his problems, on the surface at least, quite lightly. Similarly, George Eliot's letters to her friends once more became a little subdued, her words edging towards the depressive, when latterly her correspondence had been filled with the lightness Lewes had brought into her life, even if the true nature of their love for each other was not specifically referenced. In a letter to Mrs Bray, dated Saturday, 18 April 1854, George Eliot wrote:

> I am rather overdone with this week's work, and the prospect
> of what is to come next. Poor Lewes is ill, and is ordered
> not to put pen to paper for a month: so I have something

to do for him in addition to my own work, which is rather pressing. He is gone to Arthur Helps in Hampshire for ten days, and I really hope this total cessation from work, in obedience to a peremptory order, will end in making him better than he has been for the last year. No opera and no fun for me for the next month. Happily I shall have no time to regret it. Plenty of bright sun on your anemone bed. How lovely your place must look, with its fresh leaves!

At this point George Eliot was living at 21 Cambridge Street, Hyde Park Square, having been forced to take rooms there in October 1853. She began to find the atmosphere at 142 the Strand too claustrophobic and inhibiting, particularly as her relationship with Lewes grew more serious. The Chapmans were not a couple who would be prepared to look away before commenting on their lodger's actions and for the sake of discretion, a move became necessary.

George Eliot's mood appeared not to have lifted by the time of her next letter to Cara Bray, when she wrote:

My troubles are purely physical – self-dissatisfaction, and despair of achieving anything worth the doing. I can truly say they vanish into nothing before any fear for the happiness of those I love. Thank you for letting me know how things are, for indeed I could not bear to be shut out from your anxieties. When I spoke of myself as an island, I did not mean that I was so exceptionally. We are all islands –

"Each in his hidden sphere of joy or woe
Our hermit spirits dwell and roam apart." –

And this seclusion is sometimes the most intensely felt at the very moment your friend is caressing or consoling you. But this gradually becomes a source of satisfaction instead of repining. When we are young we think our troubles a mighty business – that the world is spread out expressly as a stage for the particular drama of our lives, and that we have a right to rant and foam at the mouth if we are crossed. I have done enough of that in my time. But we begin at last to understand that these things are important only to our own consciousness, which is but as a globule of dew on a rose-leaf, that at mid-day there will be no trace of. This is no high flown sentimentality, but a simple reflection, which I find useful to me every day. I expect to see Mr Lewes back again to-day. His poor head – his only fortune – is not well yet; and he has the misery of being ennuye with idleness, without perceiving the compensating physical improvement. Still, I hope the good he has been getting has been greater than he has been conscious of. I expect "Feuerbach" will all be in print by the end of next week, and there are no skippings, except as have been made on very urgent grounds.

(*George Eliot's Life, Volume One*, J W Cross)

It is a testament to George Eliot's academic rigour and dedication to others that in spite of everything she was going through both physically and emotionally, not only was she was still unable to ignore her work commitments, but also that her first concern seems to have been for others, for Lewes and 'his poor head' and 'the happiness of those I love'. Her commission to translate Ludwig Feuerbach's *Das Wesen des Christentums* (*The Essence of Christianity*) from German into English had been given by John Chapman, and the work both sustained and emotionally nourished George Eliot through some turbulent months. Unlike her translation of Strauss, which ultimately had taken its toll on her health, Feuerbach's work brought comfort when it was most needed. This was mainly because his view on relationships closely aligned with those of both herself and Lewes, and because he believed, just as they did, that it was not the legality of a contract that secured the nature of true love and marriage, but the power of the actual relationship, regardless of paperwork and religious documentation.

Life abroad

Matters came to a head in the summer of 1854 when the couple realised they could no longer afford to procrastinate. If they were to move forward with their relationship and spend time living together as if married, then their move to Germany needed to happen. Although as a woman George Eliot was undoubtedly taking the biggest risk in leaving friends and family in England to live abroad with a married man, she was not the only one to fear the consequences of such a relocation. Lewes loved her, and he did not enjoy the prospect of her reputation being torn to shreds should their living arrangements be scrutinised unfairly. Nevertheless, on 20 July 1854, George Eliot wrote the following letter to her old friends, the Brays, confirming plans she had only previously hinted at to Charles Bray:

> Dear Friends – all three – I have only time to say goodbye, and God bless you. Poste Restante, Weimar, for the next six weeks, and afterwards Berlin.

In her journal entry for the same date, she records her final moments in London and the beginning of her life with Lewes:

> I said a last farewell to Cambridge Street on 20th July, 1854, and found myself on board the Ravensbourne, bound for Antwerp. The day was glorious and our passage perfect. The sunset was lovely but still lovelier the dawn as we were passing up the Scheldt between two and three in the morning. The crescent moon, the stars, the first faint blush of the dawn reflected in the glassy river, the dark mass of clouds on the horizon which sent forth flashes of lightning, and the graceful forms of the boats and sailing-vessels, painted in jet-black on the reddish gold of the sky and water made up an unforgettable picture. Then the sun rose and lighted up the sleepy shores of Belgium, with their fringe of long grass, their rows of poplars, their church spires and buildings.

The couple stopped for a time in Belgium in order to undertake some sightseeing. In her journal, George Eliot recorded some of the highlights of their visit, with trips to view Rubens' *The Descent from the Cross* and *The Elevation of the Cross*. *The Descent from the Cross* forms part of a triptych alongside *The Elevation of the Cross*, which at the time of their visit had been undergoing restoration. Situated in the Cathedral of Our Lady in Antwerp, George Eliot was obviously impressed by the beauty of the images, recording her reaction to them in her journal as follows:

> The great treat at Antwerp was the sight of the Descent from the Cross, which with its pendant, the Elevation of the Cross, has been undergoing restoration. In the latter the face of Jesus is sublime in its expression of agony and trust in the Divine. It is certainly the finest conception of the suffering of Christ I have ever seen. The rest of the picture gave me no pleasure. But in the Descent from the Cross, colour, form and expression alike impressed me with the sense of grandeur and beauty. A little miserable copy of the picture placed near it served as an admirable foil.

However, it seems that memories from home were never far away, and that the opportunity to truly escape from life in London was still eluding the couple. Whilst having breakfast at the public rooms in a hotel in Cologne at the end of July, the couple were forced to invite none other than Dr Brabant and David Friedrich Strauss to join them, after having been somewhat besieged by Dr Brabant on a railway platform whilst continuing their journey from Antwerp to Cologne. George Eliot commented only briefly on this in her journal, remarking that they had a 'short interview with them'. It is easy to imagine the stilted conversation and discomfort caused by such a meeting, and the couple must have wondered if they were ever going to be able to start afresh without ties from the past hindering new possibilities. In spite of this brief interlude of concern, George Eliot and Lewes were determined to stick to their plans, and they continued to travel throughout Germany. Their wanderings took them to Coblenz and Frankfurt. Lewes was intent upon writing a book about Goethe, and staying near Frankfurt gave him an opportunity to be close to the house the writer had lived in when he was young.

From Frankfurt, the couple made their way to Weimar, from where they took an excursion to Ettersburg, a summer residence of the Duke of Weimar. Not only were provisions taken but also a copy of Keats's poetry and it is easy to imagine them lounging on rugs, eating and reading poetry to each other. George Eliot was particularly impressed with the duke's residence, commenting in her journal on its 'moderate size' and its lack of 'pretension':

> Two flights of stairs lead up to the door, and the balustrades are ornamented with beautiful creepers. A tiny sort of piazza under the steps is ornamented with creepers too, and has pretty earthenware vases filled with plants hanging from the ceiling.

Meeting Liszt

Perhaps one of the highlights of the couple's travels was their meeting with Franz Liszt. George Eliot in particular felt herself transformed by the sheer power and beauty of his music, but there was something else which drew her towards the composer. Twice in his life, Liszt had lived with women he loved but had been unable to marry. In the early 1830s he had begun a relationship with the already-married Countess Marie d'Agoult. By 1835, the countess had left her husband and family and was living with Liszt in Geneva – their daughter Blandine was born there in December. They were together for the next four years and spent their time between Italy and Switzerland. Their second daughter, Cosima, was born in Como and in 1839, their first son and third child, Daniel, was born in Paris. However, by the end of that year, their relationship deteriorated and whilst Liszt began to tour once more, the countess settled in Paris. They spent holidays with their children but in essence, their life as a couple was over.

In 1847, while performing in a concert in Kiev, Liszt met a Polish princess. Carolyne zu Sayn-Wittgenstein played a pivotal role in her lover's life as she convinced him to turn his attentions to composing. For the next twelve years, Liszt dedicated his time to his own compositions. The princess lived with him and was his constant companion. Although the couple wished to marry, their plans were thwarted not only because her husband was still alive, but also because the Catholic church refused to believe her marriage to him had been invalid.

Witnessing such a genius as Liszt living the life she herself wanted gave George Eliot hope that it was possible to be fulfilled creatively whilst also living with a loved one, even without the bonds of marriage that Victorian society seemed to demand. Her journal entries are full of praise for him, 'Liszt's conversation is charming. I never met with a person whose manner of telling a story is so piquant,' and 'Liszt's replies were always felicitous and characteristic,' as well as:

> I sat next to Liszt, and my great delight was to watch him and observe the sweetness of his expression. Genius, benevolence and tenderness beam from his whole countenance, and his manners are in perfect harmony with it. Then came the thing I had longed for – his playing. I sat near him, so that I could see both his hands and his face. For the first time in my life I beheld real inspiration – for the first time I heard the true tones of his piano.

Not only was George Eliot able to be inspired by Liszt's playing, but she no doubt took inspiration from the fact that other people were in the room listening to his music alongside her and Lewes. In spite of his living arrangements, the composer was not a social pariah. He had not been cast aside by society, and this certainly must have given them hope that one day, they too could live openly in Britain without having to worry about the scandal their situation might arouse.

Although the couple were certainly enjoying their time travelling, firstly in Belgium and then Germany, there was also work to be completed, and not just Lewes's research in preparation for his book on Goethe. It was important that both Lewes and George Eliot made money during their time abroad, not simply to sustain themselves. Agnes was still dependent on Lewes for an income for both herself and their children, and as he was legally still married to her, he was required to pay for their upkeep. This resulted in him writing his usual articles for the *Leader* and the payment he should have received was instead directly paid to Agnes. It was George Eliot who suffered greatest from a lack of confidence in her abilities while they were travelling. Little mention had been made of her Feuerbach translation since its publication, and her only solace was to be found in helping Lewes with his research on Goethe. She read Goethe's work and translated German passages into English – the nearest she came to fulfilling the role of a Dorothea-type helpmate. Although Lewes could in no way be considered an inspiration for the pedant Casaubon, in George Eliot's willingness to be considered useful, there is a certain likeness to Dorothea Brooke's wish to break away from typical stereotypes and be practical and useful in a way women were not usually allowed to be:

'I should learn everything, then,' she said to herself, still walking quickly along the bridle road through the wood. 'It would be my duty to study that I might help him the better in his great works. There would be nothing trivial about our lives. Everyday-things with us would mean the greatest things. It would be like marrying Pascal. I should learn to see the truth by the same light as great men have seen it by. And then I should know what to do, when I got older: I should see how it was possible to lead a grand life here – now – in England. I don't feel sure about doing good in any way now: everything seems like going on a mission to a people whose language I don't know; – unless it were building good cottages – there can be no doubt about that. Oh, I hope I should be able to get the people well housed in Lowick! I will draw plenty of plans while I have time.'

(Book One, Chapter Three, *Middlemarch*)

Here, Dorothea is obviously much younger and much more naïve than her creator, and in believing she will be helping Casaubon in his 'great works' and that marrying him would be akin to marrying Pascal, she is woefully mistaken. Her marriage to Casaubon proves to be a disappointment as, in academic terms at least, her husband falls far short of showing the mastery and intelligence of the great seventeenth-century mathematician Blaise Pascal. The truth that Dorothea discovers is infinitely different to the one she expects to find, but as the novel progresses, so does she, and as she matures, she becomes conscious of the nature of true happiness. Dorothea is most akin to George Eliot in her need to lead a 'grand life' and to accomplish tasks which could be considered to be more than 'trivial'. It was this urge to produce work that George Eliot was beginning to miss whilst travelling abroad. She was happier than ever before and had found love with a soulmate who not only met her expectations, but who fully deserved her love in return. However, this apparently came at a price because for the first time in many months, she was unable to produce the articles and reviews that also allowed her to feel true satisfaction.

One small glimmer of light came in the form of an opportunity given to her by Lewes to translate some work by the seventeenth-century Dutch philosopher Baruch Spinoza. The publisher Bohn had initially contracted Lewes to complete the task, but he was now so deeply immersed in his book on Goethe that he asked George Eliot to complete the work for him. She gladly agreed, relishing the opportunity to once more do something of value, and to engage with an enlightened thinker who had embroiled himself in biblical criticism. The offer of work came at the right time and not just for economic reasons. After eight months of living abroad as if married, the couple were to return to Britain. They realised it was impossible to hide away in other countries forever, however much contentment this might have brought them and it was important for both that money was made from the work they produced. Perhaps even more essential was the fact that they needed to find stimulating commissions to complete in order to remain academically fulfilled. Ultimately, they felt they had little choice but to move back to Britain for this to happen, and in particular to retain their links to London, which after all, was still very much the cultural and literary capital of not just Britain, but also Europe.

Returning to Britain

In March 1855, George Eliot and Lewes made the return trip by boat back to Britain, after having spent the final part of their trip sightseeing in Berlin. Lewes needed to go to London to settle affairs with Agnes and to spend time with the children he had gone eight months without seeing. Meanwhile, George Eliot took lodgings in 1 Sydney Place, Dover, where she was forced to spend over a month alone, with only her reading material, her journal and Spinoza's *Ethics* for company. Her journal entry for 15 March appears to show her in good spirits:

> A lovely day. As I walked up the Castle hill this afternoon the town, with its background of softly rounded hills shrouded in sleepy haze, its little lines of water looking golden in the sun, made a charming picture. I have written the preface to the Third Book of "Ethics", read Scherr, and Shakespeare's "Venus and Adonis".

Reading material and letters

She was doing as she had always done – reading, focusing on her academic work, and walking in the fresh air in order to keep up her morale. The following day, she passed her time in much the same way:

> I read Shakespeare's "Passionate Pilgrim" at breakfast and found a sonnet in which he expresses admiration of Spenser (sonnet viii):
> "Dowland to thee is dear, whose heavenly touch
> Upon the lute doth ravish human sense;
> Spenser to me, whose conceit is such
> As, passing all conceit needs no defence.
> I must send word of this to G, who has written in his "Goethe" that Shakespeare has left no line in praise of a contemporary. I could not resist the temptation of walking out before I sat down to work. Came in at half past ten, and translated Spinoza till nearly one. Walked out again till two. After dinner read "Two Gentlemen of Verona", and some of the "Sonnets". That play disgusted me more than ever in the final scene where Valentine, on Proteus's mere begging pardon, when he has no longer any hope of gaining his ends, says, "All that was mine in Sylvia, I give thee!" Silvia standing by. Walked up the castle hill again, and came in at six. Read Scherr, and found an important hint that I have made a mistake in a sentence of my article on "Austria" about the death of Franz von Sickingen.

George Eliot must have been missing Lewes terribly. She had gone from spending almost every minute of the past eight months with him, to being almost completely isolated in her lodgings in Dover. Even worse, he was now in London and she was removed from the discord their elopement might have caused, meaning she was certain to be anxious about any repercussions Lewes would be facing. She might even have been wondering about his constancy and faithfulness, and this may have compelled her to be slightly more critical of Shakespeare's *Two Gentlemen of Verona* than she otherwise would have been. In the play, Proteus has been in love with Julia, but upon seeing Silvia, who is loved by his best friend Valentine, he falls instantly in love and dismisses all thoughts of Julia. When Proteus makes his feelings known to Silvia she rejects him, and so instead he threatens rape. It is Valentine who prevents this happening, and his actions force Proteus

133

to realise how appalling his actions have become. Having witnessed his repentance, and believing it to be genuine, Valentine appears to offer Silvia to him, 'All that was mine in Silvia I give thee'. However, a more modern interpretation is that Valentine means only that he wishes to give the same amount of love he has for Silvia to Proteus as a sign of forgiveness, and not that he wishes to offer up Silvia herself. It is easy to understand why George Eliot interpreted the line in the way she did. Secluded and shut away from society as she was, it would not be difficult to believe the worst: that men could share women and in so doing define them as objects.

It is interesting, therefore, to note how George Eliot filled her days with walking, fresh air and reading, as well as her translation work and journal entries. Correspondence to and from friends and loved ones must have become increasingly important, so it comes as no surprise that in her letter to Cara Bray's sister, Sara Hennell, written on 16 March 1855, she asks for news of everyone at Rosehill:

> I dare say you will be surprised to see that I write from Dover. We left Berlin on the 11th. I have taken lodgings here for a little while, until Mr Lewes has concluded some arrangements in London; and, with the aid of lovely weather, am even enjoying my solitude, though I don't mind how soon it ends. News of you all at Rosehill – how health, and business and all other things are faring – would be very welcome to me, if you can find time for a little note of homely details. I am well and calmly happy – feeling much stronger and clearer in mind for the last eight months of new experience. We were very sorry to leave our quiet rooms and agreeable friends in Berlin, though the place itself is certainly ugly and *am Ende* must become terribly wearisome for those who have not a vocation there. We went again and again to the new museum to look at the casts of the Parthenon sculptures, and registered a vow that we would go to feast on the sight of the originals the first day we could spare in London. I had never cast more than a fleeting look on them before but now I can in some degree understand the effect they produced on their first discovery.

George Eliot's letters are full of good spirits at this time, and it gives the reader cause to wonder. Was she as happy as she seemed to be maintaining? The joy she had found through her love for Lewes, which for once was mutual and reciprocated, had been temporarily taken from her. Her walks and reading might have kept her occupied, but she had grown used to sharing these with someone who appreciated her comments and thoughts. The joy she must have felt at returning time and time again to the museum in Berlin, and the pact they had made as a couple to visit the original Parthenon sculptures at the British Museum, no doubt seemed like a lifetime away. She had waited for so many years to find someone who appreciated her for who she was, and now Lewes's marital status, and moreover, society's preoccupation with it, was preventing them being together. Her frustration and anguish surely became unbearable at times. However, a few days later she received a note from John Chapman, asking her to oversee part of the Contemporary Literature section of the *Westminster Review*. Such correspondence must have come as something as a relief. Not only was she being offered paid work, but it also suggested that not all of their friends had abandoned the couple.

It was not until 18 April that George Eliot and George Henry Lewes were once more reunited. Initially, they moved into rooms in Bayswater while searching for accommodation that was in keeping with their tastes and needs. Less than a week later they had secured lodgings at 7 Clarence Row, East Sheen, although they were unable to move in until 2 May. In the meantime, and over the next few months, George Eliot kept herself busy with the commissioned work she had managed to secure, as her journal entries make clear:

> April 28th – Finished article on Weimar for Fraser.
> May 28th – Sent Belles-lettres section to Westminster Review. During May several articles written for the Leader.
> June 13th – Began Part IV of Spinoza's "Ethics".
> June 21st – Finished article on Brougham's "Lives of Men of Letters".

On 25 April 1855 the couple also delivered on their promise to visit the British Museum, and when not working, George Eliot continued to expand her knowledge by reading a diverse range of material. In her journal she recorded both the fiction and non-fiction that engaged her. This included a variety of plays by Shakespeare, such as *Macbeth*, *The Tempest*, *Richard II* and *Henry VI*, an article on Dryden, and Schrader's *German Mythology*, which she recorded as being a 'poor book'.

George Eliot's confidence should have been on the rise. Lewes had managed to secure them accommodation, she was still able to find work for herself and much to her joy, there were friends who were liberal-minded enough not to cut them out of their lives and cast them as social miscreants. They were visited not only by Charles Bray, but also by Rufa Brabant (now Rufa Hennell), and a friend of George Eliot's, Bessie Raynor Parkes. However, something always prevented George Eliot admitting openly to many people that she and Lewes were not married, and throughout the decades this has given some feminists cause to question her dedication to the campaign for women's liberty and suffrage.

Chapter Nine

In which George Eliot's views on the role of women in society are further scrutinised and discussed

And, of course men know best about everything, except what women know better.

(*Middlemarch*)

One of the first people to visit the couple as soon as they had established themselves in lodgings together was Bessie Raynor Parkes. Over a decade later, Bessie would marry the Frenchman Louis Belloc and go on to give birth to Joseph Hilaire Belloc, who would one day become a famous writer, but for now she was engaged to Sam Blackwell, and would remain so for ten years.

Bessie Raynor Parkes

Bessie had been lucky to receive a progressive education at her Unitarian boarding school. Her parents were wealthy and she had been exposed to culture, literature and the arts from quite a young age. As she grew older, she became much more aware of the hypocrisy and double standards that society exhibited towards women, and of the patriarchal nature of the ruling classes. Along with a mutual friend of George Eliot's – Barbara Leigh Smith Bodichon – she tried to change the restrictive property laws that married women were forced to abide by, and joined a group called the Committee for the Ladies' Address to their American Sisters on Slavery, in a bid to show her animosity towards the American South's slave trade. She was also an advocate for equality in female education, believing girls had every right to receive as fully and as rounded an education as boys. Like George Eliot, Bessie Raynor Parkes was interested in writing and literature. She was one of a group of women who felt galvanised enough by the women's liberation movement to help set up a journal – *The English Women's Journal* – specifically for the purposes of allowing females a space to write about their experiences of fighting for suffrage and equality, and to promote the cause of liberation even further.

In spite of her obvious support for George Eliot, Bessie did cause her friend some difficulty. When calling upon her in lodgings, or when writing to her, she often forgot to use the name George Eliot now insisted everyone use when addressing her: Mrs Lewes. Bessie compounded the problem further by using George Eliot's maiden name, and also by using the term 'Miss'. This not only caused confusion for George Eliot and Lewes's landlady, but could have caused her to become suspicious about a couple she had rented rooms to in the belief that they were married. George Eliot continuously reminded Bessie that she was only to be referred to as Mrs Lewes. Perhaps Bessie's forgetfulness says more about her own situation in life and the feelings of many other women who were finding life living under the watchful eye of the patriarchal establishment difficult, than it does about her view on George Eliot's decision to live as if married when she was not.

Bessie was engaged, but there is a chance her heart was not completely committed to the relationship – an idea which seems to be fully borne out by the fact that she and her fiancé Sam Blackwell never married. Her father, Joseph Parkes, tried to ban her from visiting the Leweses, a ban which she bravely defied, in spite of the fact that her father tried convincing her that Lewes was a cad, and therefore unworthy of her friend's love. It was not until Bessie actually met with Lewes that she was fully convinced he was a suitable partner for her friend.

Some feminists would have preferred George Eliot to be honest about her situation and to promote the cause of divorce and highlight all that was wrong with the legal system by insisting on living openly with Lewes as his wife, yet at the same time maintaining her status as a single woman. This would no doubt have caused the couple and their families considerable pain, and allowed the wider world to comment on their situation without them having any control over the matter. After all, many of their social circle and beyond already knew that the Leweses were not legally married, but by insisting on the name Mrs Lewes, George Eliot was upholding her own personal beliefs – something which was of extreme importance to her. In the nineteenth century, women could still be resolutely tied to men for whom they felt no love simply because their fathers insisted the marriage was a suitable one. Thus, many legal marriages were unhappy ones. George Eliot's partnership with Lewes was one of free choice and of love and fulfilment. To her, their relationship was an example of what marriage was always intended to be and, therefore, on moral grounds alone, she decided she had every right to be called Mrs Lewes. With this thought in mind, it is possible to claim that George Eliot's insistence on being called Mrs Lewes had less to do with her denial of a woman's rights or her lack of courage in the face of society's disdain, and more to do with her irrevocable conviction in her own beliefs regarding marriage. She saw marriage as being an act between two people who loved, honoured and respected each other. Without such feelings she believed marriage meant nothing, regardless of its legal status or having been solemnised by the church, and so by entering willingly into a relationship with Lewes, she believed she was the closest he would ever come to having a true and honest wife, and that theirs was a loving and respectful 'marriage'.

Silly novels

George Eliot was a woman who never suffered fools gladly, whether they be men or women, and she was always very honest in her views on a person regardless of their gender. In an article published anonymously for the *Westminster Review* in October 1856, she lamented the sort of novels some women were either likely to read, or even worse, write themselves:

> Silly Novels by Lady Novelists are a genus with many species, determined by the particular quality of silliness

that predominates in – the frothy, the prosy, the pious, or the pedantic. But it is a mixture of all these – a composite order of feminine fatuity, that produces the largest class of such novels, which we shall distinguish as the mind-and-military species. The heroine is usually an heiress, probably a peeress in her own right, with perhaps a vicious baronet, an amiable duke, and an irresistible younger son of a marquis as lovers in the foreground, a clergyman and a poet sighing for her in the middle distance, and a crowd of undefined adorers dimly indicated beyond.

One of the things which appears to annoy George Eliot about this type of novel is their lack of realism. In much the same way as modern magazines present the twenty-first century reader with unrealistic and unattainable body shapes, so too did these nineteenth-century novels seem to suggest that most women should expect to have at least a dozen suitors in order to be considered a success in life. Not only did George Eliot have first-hand and painful experience of this not being the case, but she also realised how damaging it could be for a young woman to consider her number of suitors a sign of success. Like her friends Bessie Raynor Parkes and Barbara Leigh Smith Bodichon, George Eliot wanted women to feel proud of their success in education, in their grasp of knowledge and in the skills they developed, not simply in how adept they were in capturing the attention of the opposite sex. She was also scathing in how many of these novels seemed to present their heroines as beautiful, gracious and talented in the skills valued above all others by Victorian gentlemen:

> Her eyes and her wit are both dazzling; her nose and her morals are alike free from any tendency to irregularity; she has a superb contralto and a superb intellect; she is perfectly well-dressed and perfectly religious; she dances like a sylph, and reads the Bible in the original tongues. Or it may be that the heiress is not an heiress – that rank and wealth are the only things in which she is deficient; but she infallibly gets into high society, she has the triumph of refusing many matches and securing the best, and she wears some family jewels or other as a sort of crown of righteousness at the

end. Rakish men either bite their lips in impotent confusion at her repartees, or are touched to penitence by her reproofs, which on appropriate occasions, rise to a lofty strain of rhetoric; indeed, there is a general propensity in her to make speeches, and to rhapsodize at some length when she retires to her bedroom.

This is a gloriously indignant piece of commentary on the type of heroine typically presented to female readers in the middle of the nineteenth century. The heroines to be found in these novels, according to George Eliot, have reached unparalleled levels of perfection, and even without an inheritance will always somehow end up living among the rich. George Eliot's caustic wit helps the reader understand how much she despised such caricatures, knowing full well many ordinary women of the time would be unable to achieve similar good fortune. The lack of realism displayed afforded George Eliot little pleasure. She gives the example of Henrietta Georgiana Marcia Lascelles's *Compensation: A Story of Real Life Thirty Years Ago*, which was published in 1856. In the novel, a child of 4 speaks with so much grandeur that George Eliot is forced to wonder if the writer has ever met a child of such a young age, concluding with wonderment:

> There are few women, we suppose, who have not seen something of children under five years of age.

This leads her to ponder, therefore, why Lascelles should be so inaccurate in her rendition of such a young child's speech, and concludes this is why the youngster's mother is constantly referred to as a genius. The dialogue spoken by the 4-year-old proves that realism was indeed far from Lascelles' mind when she wrote it:

> 'Oh I am so happy, dear gran'mamma; – I have seen, – I have seen such a delightful person: he is like everything beautiful, – like the smell of sweet flowers and the view of Ben Lomond; – or no, better than that – he is like what I think of and see when I am very, very happy; and he is really like mamma, too, when she sings; and his

forehead is like that distant sea,' she continued, pointing to the blue Mediterranean; 'there seems no end – no end; or like the cluster of stars I like best to look at on a warm fine night...Don't look so... your forehead is like Loch Lomond, when the wind is blowing and the sun is gone in.'

Such similes indeed are impressive when used by a 4-year-old – especially when they are mostly used to describe an individual's forehead! Although George Eliot was aware of the comedic elements in the overwriting involved in these 'silly novels', she was also concerned about the dangerous message that could be sent to impressionable or naïve young readers.

Women with the beliefs of George Eliot, Bessie Raynor Parkes and Barbara Leigh Smith Bodichon wanted other women to believe they were worth more than their facial appearance, fine figures, and feminine charms. They wanted literature that promoted the value of education, morals and knowledge over and above fine clothes and a delicate appearance. In her essay, *Silly Novels by Lady Novelists*, George Eliot was concerned that much of the reading matter written by women, or that was produced for women, insisted on promoting clichés, plots and characters which were unrealistic. Indeed, many of them seemed to have a fairy tale quality, suggesting they were more suitable for children than fully grown adults who were simultaneously expected to rear children and run households. Even worse, if the heroines in such novels were well-educated, their knowledge was used against them and they were portrayed as insufferably boring and far too smug and self-satisfied, something the novels hinted wryly, a real-life lady should avoid at all costs. The only female novelists George Eliot promotes in her essay are Currer Bell (Charlotte Brontë), Mrs Gaskell, and Harriet Martineau, believing they extolled valuable ideas or that they created the sort of heroine female readers should try to emulate.

George Eliot examined similar ideas in her own novels, where she was careful to include female protagonists who might either inspire her readers or who could present them with a valuable lesson on how not to behave. *Middlemarch* gives us a fascinating study of two such women in the guise of Dorothea Brooke and Rosamond Vincy.

Dorothea and Rosamond

Dorothea Brooke is only 19 at the beginning of the novel and although she is undoubtedly naïve at times, no-one can fault her determination to do good in the world. Interestingly, in spite of being beautiful, she does not spend time or money on her clothing, believing there are more important things in life to consider:

> Miss Brooke had that kind of beauty which seems to be thrown into light relief by poor dress. Her hand and wrist were so finely formed that she could wear sleeves not less bare of style than those in which the Blessed Virgin appeared to Italian painters; and her profile as well as her stature and bearing seemed to gain the more dignity from her plain garments, which by the side of provincial fashion gave her the impressiveness of a fine quotation from the Bible – or from one of our elder poets, – in a paragraph of today's newspaper.
>
> (Book One, Chapter One, *Middlemarch*)

She is described as being 'remarkably clever', with the caveat that her sister Celia is generally regarded as having more common-sense. She has opened a school for infants in the nearby village and wants, among other things, to redesign the local workers' cottages, something which Celia refers to as a 'fad':

> 'Poor Dodo,' she went on, in an amiable staccato. 'It is very hard: it is your favourite *fad* to draw plans.'
> '*Fad* to draw plans! Do you think I only care about my fellow-creatures' houses in that childish way? I may well make mistakes. How can one ever do anything nobly Christian, living among people with such petty thoughts?'
>
> (Book One, Chapter Four, *Middlemarch*)

Dorothea is irritated by her sister's belief that her interest in planning the workers' cottages is done from mere amusement. She is intent upon doing good, and upon making the lives of the tenant farmers as easy as she can by improving their homes. Dorothea's determination to do good continues throughout *Middlemarch,* and even in disappointment she strives to balance her feelings by striving to help others. When she realises Casaubon is not the man she thought he was – and certainly not a great academic – and that his interest in helping the workers is only superficial, she is able to forgive him:

> But was not Mr Casaubon just as learned as before? Had his forms of expression changed, or his sentiments become less laudable? O waywardness of womanhood! Did his chronology fail him, or his ability to state not only a theory but the names of those who held it; or his provision for giving the heads of any subject on demand? And was not Rome the place in all the world to give free play to such accomplishments? Besides, had not Dorothea's enthusiasm especially dwelt on the prospect of relieving the weight and perhaps the sadness with which great tasks lie on him who has to achieve them? – And that such weight pressed on Mr Casaubon was only plainer than before.
>
> (Book Two, Chapter Twenty, *Middlemarch*)

Here the intervention of George Eliot's gently chiding authorial voice comes after Dorothea has been sobbing on her honeymoon in Rome, without being able to explain why. The writer's intention to add realism to her novels means that Dorothea has gradually become aware that her marriage to Casaubon is not all she thought it would be. George Eliot is only pointing out what the reader has probably already realised – that Casaubon is not the right husband for a beautiful 19-year-old girl who wishes only to do good, but who has not yet had enough experience of the world to understand she will need a younger, more outward-looking husband to help her succeed in her mission.

As a counter-balance to Dorothea, George Eliot introduces Rosamond Vincy to her readers. Rosamond's beauty is different to Dorothea's in that she is aware of it, and actively cultivates it for the benefit of others. She is described as having:

> excellent taste in costume, with that nymph-like figure and pure blondness which gave the largest range to choice in the flow and colour of drapery. But these things made

only part of her charm. She was admitted to be the flower of Mrs Lemon's school, the chief school in the county, where the teaching included all that was demanded in the accomplished female – even to extras, such as the getting in and out of a carriage. Mrs Lemon herself had always held up Miss Vincy as an example: no pupil, she said, exceeded that young lady for mental acquisition and propriety of speech, while her musical execution was quite exceptional.

(Book One, Chapter Eleven, *Middlemarch*)

Unfortunately, Miss Vincy has seemingly left school with little knowledge of the accomplishments that are really important in life. She is interested only in supercilious acquisitions, such as material possessions, and when she is eventually married to Dr Lydgate, her determination to own pretty china and dresses will eventually financially and morally bankrupt them. Rosamond's life is a performance, something she has been taught at Mrs Lemon's school, where even getting in and out of a carriage is a feature of her education. George Eliot is keen to point out that Rosamond is the product of an education system which has emphasised the priority of appearance and performance over knowledge, and of a society which is gradually growing more obsessed with the ability to purchase objects. Rosamond does not intentionally try to hurt people; she is simply not aware enough of their feelings and their own needs. When she and Lydgate are forced to move to London at the end of the novel, Lydgate is able to acquire wealth through his work, 'having written a treatise on Gout, a disease which has a good deal of wealth on its side,' but ultimately, he considers himself a failure. Rosamond's desire for possessions has ultimately caused the couple's initial downfall, but she is blind to her own faults and unable to see the unhappiness her actions have caused:

As the years went on he opposed her less and less, whence Rosamond concluded that he had learned the value of her opinion; on the other hand, she had a more thorough conviction of his talents now that he had gained a good income, and instead of the threatened cage in Bride Street provided one all flowers and gilding, fit for the bird of paradise that she resembled. In brief, Lydgate was what is called a successful man. But he died prematurely of diphtheria, and Rosamond afterwards married an elderly and wealthy physician, who took kindly to her four children. She made a very pretty show with her daughters, driving out in her carriage, and often spoke of her happiness as a 'reward' – she did not say for what, but probably she meant that it was a reward for her patience with Tertius, whose temper never became faultless, and to the last occasionally let slip a bitter speech which was more memorable than the signs he made of his repentance.

(Finale, *Middlemarch*)

Critics and readers alike continue to praise *Middlemarch,* along with George Eliot's other works, for the very reasons she chose to criticise many of the other novels written by or for women in the mid-nineteenth century. George Eliot filled her novels with realistic characters who had faults, as well as traits, that could be admired. She gave them psychological depth and ensured her plots were reflections of events that could happen in real life and refused to patronise her readers with traditional happy endings. Even in *Middlemarch*, when Dorothea and Will Ladislaw finally marry, Dorothea's happiness is initially compromised by her family's ill feeling. Furthermore, she loses her inheritance and her idealistic dreams are somewhat thwarted, but if Dorothea does not manage to change the whole of society for the better, she does at least manage to have a positive impact on those closest to her:

Her finely-touched spirit had still its fine issues, though they were not widely visible. Her full nature, like that river of which Cyrus broke the strength, spent itself in channels which had no great name on the earth. But the effect of her being on those around her was incalculably diffusive: for the growing good of the world is partly dependent on unhistoric acts; and that things are not so ill with you and me as they might have been, is half owing to the number who lived faithfully a hidden life, and rest in unvisited tombs.

(Finale, *Middlemarch*)

George Eliot is commending Dorothea for the small acts of kindness she committed during her lifetime, commenting that while she was unable to become sufficiently well-known for people to visit her tomb, she would become one of the honourable people that many came to rely upon for acts of goodness and charity.

Some readers believe Dorothea deserved to be rewarded with more than marriage to Will Ladislaw, in spite of her love for him, and some feminists in particular believe that if George Eliot had left Miss Brooke as a single woman, or at least portrayed her as refusing to undertake a second marriage after Casaubon's death, then she would have been an excellent example for single women who wished to pursue a life for themselves other than a married one. However, George Eliot considered herself married to Lewes and spent some of her happiest and most fulfilled years while in partnership with the man she regarded as her soulmate. Therefore, it makes sense for her to reflect these feelings in *Middlemarch*, and for Dorothea to achieve happiness through her own marriage to Will. George Eliot found it possible to achieve both personal and professional success and believed that if they so wished to, others could do the same. Perhaps ultimately, her search for personal happiness eclipsed her desire to fight for the cause of feminism, and this is what might have led feminist readers to challenge some of the ideas she appeared to hold sacred, especially those she promoted in her novels.

Many of the heroines in George Eliot's novels appear to live a life which is the antithesis of their creator, and this is probably what has disappointed feminists throughout the decades. In *Romola*, the eponymous heroine plans to abandon her husband in order to achieve the academic learning she yearns for. However, upon leaving him, she is never bold enough to fulfil her desire and returns to her husband determined to be reunited with him. In *Adam Bede,* Dinah Morris, a Methodist and a lay preacher at a time when it was believed no woman should take it upon herself to speak the word of God, even if only from a village green, gives up her desire to minister to others and marries Adam, apparently happy with the decision she has made to conform to society's expectations. Although she does indeed love Adam, first she needs to convince herself that by marrying him, she is fulfilling God's wishes for her:

> 'Adam,' she said, 'it is the Divine Will. My soul is so knit to yours that it is but a divided life I live without you. And this moment, now you are with me, and I feel that

our hearts are filled with the same love, I have a fullness of strength to bear, and do our heavenly Father's Wil', that I had lost before.'

(Chapter Fifty-Four, Adam Bede)

In *Silas Marner,* Nancy Lammeter is a woman who embraces inactivity. Life appears to happen to Nancy, and she lives by an inflexible code from which she will not stray. As much as she longs for a child, she refuses to adopt one in case she defies God's plan, and thus she remains unhappily childless. Her inability to be proactive and challenge her own code ensures aspects of her life remain filled with sorrow:

> It was one of those rigid principles, and no petty egoistic feeling, which had been the ground of Nancy's difficult resistance to her husband's wish. To adopt a child, because children of your own had been denied you, was to try and choose your lot in spite of Providence: the adopted child, she was convinced, would never turn out well, and would be a curse to those who had wilfully and rebelliously sought what it was clear that, for some high reason, they were better without. When you saw a thing was not meant to be, said Nancy, it was a bounden duty to leave off so much as wishing for it.

(Part Two, Chapter Seventeen, Silas Marner)

Some readers believe that George Eliot wrote about women in this way because she did not want to make her own gender apparent to her wider readership. Adopting a male pseudonym was no guarantee that her true identity or gender would remain a secret forever, but by creating female characters who had faults that women themselves might disagree with, she would ensure her true gender would not easily be discovered.

Ultimately, what readers and feminists have to recognise is that George Eliot was never really a campaigner. First and foremost, she was a writer, and her own personal situation did not make her any more likely to decide whether or not women needed to have the vote. In fact, the evidence suggests she believed they did not, in spite of the fact that she lived a life away from many of the patriarchal restrictions that caused women to demand the vote in the first place. In *Felix Holt: The Radical,* elections are depicted as violent and troubled, where, 'The confused deafening shouts, the incidental fighting, the knocking over, pulling and scuffling, seemed to increase every moment,' (p.311), and there is more than a hint of corruption.

Some readers have been keen to point out that those women in her novels who have behaved badly in some way, or have fallen foul of society's expectations, are often punished. Hetty Sorrel, for example, commits infanticide and faces the death penalty before finally being transported to Australia; Maggie Tulliver's intelligence and her passion for Stephen Guest are rewarded with death; while Dinah Morris is forced to give up the preaching for which she shows such aptitude and skill. However, as readers, we also have to recognise that George Eliot was far too clever a writer to simply see her female characters in terms of good and bad. What she was able to do was recognise the reasons why they had behaved in the way they did, and it was this understanding that added psychological depth to her novels.

Hetty Sorrel

George Eliot was always keen to encourage her readers to look beyond her characters' personality traits when it came to apportioning blame for their actions, and in her writing, she forces us to examine their upbringing, their living arrangements and their education. Hetty Sorrel, for example, has been abandoned with an illegitimate child, and there are times when she seems hardly able to look after herself, let alone another infant. She is only 17 at the start of the novel, and her vanity and selfishness are counterbalanced by her lack of natural intelligence and education. She is easily taken advantage of and therefore, the reader finds it easy to feel pity for her in spite of her negative qualities:

> Poor wandering Hetty, with the rounded childish face, and the hard unloving despairing soul looking out of it – with the narrow heart and narrow thoughts, no room in them for any sorrows but her own, and tasting that sorrow with the more intense bitterness! My heart bleeds for her as I see her toiling along on her weary feet, or seated in a cart with her eyes fixed vacantly on the road before her, never thinking

or caring whither it tends, till hunger comes and makes her
desire that a village may be near.

What will be the end? – the end of her objectless
wandering, apart from all love, caring for human beings
only through her pride, clinging to life only as the hunted
wounded brute clings to it?

God preserve you and me from the beginnings of such
misery!

(Chapter Thirty-Seven, *Adam Bede*)

Hetty's 'rounded childish face' is George Eliot's way of reminding her
readers that Hetty is little more than a child herself, and has to face her
pregnancy alone at a time when such an event, if discovered, could lead
to total and absolute social ostracisation.

However, Hetty also transgresses society's rules in another way when
it is made clear that she has aspirations that many, at the time, would
disapprove of. She secretly wishes to be 'a grand lady, and ride in her
coach, and dress for dinner in a brocaded silk, with feathers in her hair,
and her dress sweeping the ground.':

> And Hetty's dreams were all of luxuries: to sit in a carpeted
> parlour, and always wear white stockings; to have some
> large beautiful earrings such as were all the fashion; to have
> Nottingham lace round the top of her gown, and something
> to make her handkerchief smell nice, like Miss Lydia
> Donnithorne's when she drew it out at church; and not to
> be obliged to get up early or be scolded by anybody. She
> thought, if Adam had been rich and could have given her
> these things, she loved him well enough to marry him.
>
> (Chapter Seven, *Adam Bede*)

Society at the time had strict rules which individuals were meant to
follow. The higher classes in particular had no time for those people
who tried to rise above their allotted station in life and transcend their
social class. In not only imagining herself as a lady, but in taking action
to assume the role of someone from the higher classes through pursuing
a relationship with Captain Donnithorne, Hetty would have been seen
to have transgressed these laws. George Eliot is therefore highlighting

another reason for a woman's downfall. Society's double standards will allow men from the upper classes to use women and remain relatively unscathed. Women, however, if found guilty of 'allowing themselves' to be taken advantage of are punished for their fall from grace and for allowing their own personal ambitions to have clouded their judgement.

Maggie Tulliver

Maggie Tulliver was brought up by parents who found it difficult to handle such an intelligent and independent daughter. Her mother, in particular, despairs that Maggie cannot be more like her cousin Lucy Deane, and tries to conquer Maggie's spirit along with her hair:

> 'there's her cousin Lucy's got a row o' curls round her head, an' not a hair out o' place. It seems hard as my sister Deane should have that pretty child; I'm sure Lucy takes more after me nor my own child does. Maggie, Maggie,' continued the mother, in a tone of half-coaxing fretfulness, as this small mistake of nature entered the room, 'where's the use o' my telling you to keep away from the water? You'll tumble in and be drownded someday, an' then you'll be sorry you didn't do as mother told you.'
> (Book First, Chapter Two, *The Mill on the Floss*)

The humour of Mrs Tulliver's words are overshadowed by the prophesy she unwittingly makes at the end of her speech. But Maggie does not drown simply because she is being punished for her relationship with Stephen Guest. Her upbringing means that throughout her life she was thwarted: starved of the education and experiences her natural intelligence required. Her inquisitive nature and passion pushed her to look for the new ventures that society's restrictions forced her to be excluded from. George Eliot is ultimately blaming society for Maggie's eventual demise, and is asking her readers to look beyond the minor faults of her characters and to consider the larger faults of society that were implicit in their fates. This is the message she concerned herself with in her novels, and it was adding this psychological depth and realism to her characters that interested her far more than using them as mouth-pieces for the cause of women's liberation. She was able to separate her personal life from the political in her writing and did not blame or look down upon those women who were content to be married and bring up a family. The only times George Eliot raised concerns were if those women, or indeed men, were not happily married, or were being mistreated in some way. She firmly believed everyone deserved a chance to be happy and respected in the life they lived at home.

Chapter Ten

In which George Eliot is persuaded to begin her career as a novelist

The foolish vanity of wishing to appear in print, instead of being counterbalanced by any consciousness of the intellectual or moral derogation implied in futile authorship, seems to be encouraged by the extremely false impression that to write at all is a proof of superiority in a woman.
(*Silly Novels by Silly Lady Novelists*)

In October 1855, the Leweses moved once again, this time to Park Shot, Richmond. In spite of a growing nearness to the nation's capital, it was Lewes who took the train into the city to oversee any of their business matters. George Eliot never once wanted to find herself embroiled in an embarrassing public situation where she was gossiped about, or perhaps even worse, openly ignored and snubbed in public. In time, and along with her success, the wider public became more used to her eccentric living arrangements, but in the early years neither she nor Lewes knew what reception they would receive. George Eliot was still smarting from the lack of contact she had apparently received from her old friends, the Brays. Although Charles Bray had been to visit them in spite of some old grudges he bore Lewes, letters from Rosehill had been few and far between. If this was due to any disapproval felt towards their friend's relationship with a man who was already married to someone else, it would indeed be odd considering the Brays' own marital situation, and their beliefs as radical free-thinkers. But other letters suggest there might be more to the matter than this, and that their estrangement had begun before the Leweses' move to Germany.

A troubled friendship

Cara Bray and her sister Sara were not only put out that their old friend had not confided in them more about her relationship with Lewes, but they also felt that since moving to London she had drifted away from them. This was an idea that was circulated by Charles Bray, who claimed to Sara that her friend's feelings had changed towards her. On 21 April 1852, George Eliot sought to dampen such a claim in a letter to Sara Hennell,

> If there is any change in my affection for you it is that I love you more than ever, not less. I have as perfect a friendship for you as my imperfect nature can feel – a friendship in which deep respect and admiration are sweetened by a sort of flesh – and – blood sisterly feeling and the happy consciousness that I have your affection, however unreservedly in return. I have confidence that this friendship can never be shaken; that it must last while I last and that the supposition of its ever being weakened by a momentary irritation is too absurd for me to take the trouble to deny it. As to your whole conduct to me, from the first day I knew you, it has been so generous and sympathetic that, if I did not heartily love you, I should exude deep gratitude – but love excludes gratitude. It is impossible that I should ever love two women better than I love you and Cara. Indeed, it seems to me that I can never love any so well; and it is certain that I can never have any friend – not even a husband – who would supply the loss of those associations with the past which belong to you. Do you believe in my love for you, and that it will remain as long as I have my senses, because it is interwoven with my best nature, and is dependent, not on any accident of manner, but on long experience, which has confirmed the attraction of earlier days.

George Eliot is quick to deny a change in her feelings of friendship for both Sara and Cara, claiming that nothing could ever come between them, not even a husband.

Regardless of this, however, Cara Bray and Sara Hennell believed their friend should have communicated with them more often from Germany, and they wondered why she would not have thought they would have been worried about her. To compound this idea further, the correspondence George Eliot did send tended to be addressed to Charles Bray, which hurt her two friends immeasurably. This might have been done to spare them any embarrassment regarding her move with Lewes, or because ultimately, she felt unsure of their feelings. But their friendship had been a long one, and it was not about to be torn asunder by miscommunication, embarrassment and different interpretations of the same event. Although George Eliot and Cara Bray did not see each other for several years, and she was never to visit Rosehill again, their letter-writing continued, as did their fondness for each other.

George Eliot was someone who usually spent time pondering over the tone of the letters she sent and received, and would grow particularly agitated about the language used in the missives sent to her, wondering if any words were pointedly meant to convey hurt and anger, or latterly umbrage and shock. Lewes was still visiting his other family in London, and both he and George Eliot were busy trying to find work that would sustain them both mentally and financially. Lewes was still being plagued by the headaches and ringing in his ears which had begun at the same time as his relationship with George Eliot, so a trip to the coast must have seemed like a welcome relief for them both. On 8 May 1856, the couple set out for a holiday to Ilfracombe, with Lewes eager to study and observe as closely as possible the creatures who lived along the coast. He was also impatient to put to rest an argument begun by T H Huxley, who claimed that Lewes was a second-hand biologist and merely a 'book scientist'. George Eliot was also keen to complete some articles for the *Westminster Review* and the *Leader*, while also being able to enjoy some walks in the fresh sea air. The opening of her Ilfracombe journal gives some insight into their journey to the coast:

> It was a cold unfriendly day – the eighth of May on which
> we set out for Ilfracombe, with our hamper of tall glass jars,
> which we meant for our sea-side Vivarium. We had to get

down at Windsor, and were not sorry that the interval was long enough to let us walk round the Castle, which I had never seen before, except from a distance. The famous 'slopes', the avenues in the Park and the distant landscape looked very lovely in the fresh and delicate greens of Spring, and the Castle is surely the most delightful royal residence in the world. We took our places from Windsor all the way to Exeter, having bravely made up our minds to do the greatest part of our journey in one day. At Bristol, where we had to wait three hours, the misery of my terrible headache was mitigated by the interest we felt in seeing the grand old church of St Mary Redcliffe, for ever associated with the memory of Chetterton –

It stands the maestrie of a human hand

The pride of Bristowe and the western land.

For the rest, Bristol looked dismal enough to us: a compound of dingy streets, bad smells, and dreary waiting at a dirty Railway Station.

The headaches which plagued George Eliot throughout her life had a habit of occurring at the most inopportune times, but relief was to be found at their next stop, Exeter station, where they were staying for the night. Although still hindered by her headache, on arrival at Ilfracombe the Leweses found suitable lodgings, and George Eliot recorded her initial impressions of the town. It is possible that her tiredness due to travelling, along with the pain that was still bothering her, coloured her perceptions somewhat:

There can hardly be an uglier town – an uglier cluster of nests lying in the midst of beautiful hills, than Ilfracombe. The colour of the houses is the palest, dingiest grey, and the lines are all rectangular and mean. Overtopping the whole town in ugliness as well as height are two 'Terraces', which make two factory-like lines of building on the slope of the green hill.

However, shortly afterwards there is a concession to the town's ugliness, when she writes:

156

From our windows we had a view of the higher part of the town, and generally it looked uninteresting enough; but what is it that light cannot transfigure into beauty? One evening, after a shower, as the sun was setting over the sea behind us, some peculiar arrangement of clouds threw a delicious evening light on the irregular cluster of houses and merged the ugliness of their forms in an exquisite flood of colour – as a stupid person is made glorious by a noble deed. A perfect rainbow arched over the picture.

Ilfracombe holiday

In spite of her feelings towards the town's appearance, George Eliot and Lewes continued to enjoy a fruitful holiday in Ilfracombe. Plenty of walks were taken and in her journal, George Eliot records the following:

> On clear days, I could see the Welsh Coast with the smoke of its towns very distinctly, and a good way southward the outline of Lundy Island.

By 17 June both of the articles George Eliot had been commissioned to write had been despatched, and for the first time she felt that she could truly begin to enjoy her break, without constantly worrying about the completion of her work. The Leweses alternated their time between the coast and the countryside around Ilfracombe. Sometimes they studied the sea life that was to be found in the local rock pools, and other times they wandered further afield, where they were able to revel in the beauty of the nearby woods and meadows. In her journal, George Eliot recalled all the many interesting things that were to be seen on their walk to Chambercombe, a name which originated from some nearby woods:

> G found out this walk one day and then took me there one lovely, sunshiny day. The chief beauties of the walk began when we arrived at a gate leading into a farm yard which forms a sort of ganglion to two lanes branching from it. Close to this gate there is a spring which is a perfect miniature of some Swiss 'Falls'. It spreads itself like a crystal fan on

successive ledges of the hedge-bank until it reaches a much broader ledge where it forms a little lake on a bed of brown pebbles; then down it goes again till it reaches the level of the road and runs along a tiny river. What a picture this farm yard remains in my memory! The cows staring at us with formidable timidity, such as I have sometimes seen in a human being who frightens others while he is frightened himself; and the cow-man who pointed out our way to us through the next gate. Just beyond this gate there was a little widening in the lane – several gateways occurring together and here the wild verdure and flowers of the hedgerow and the roadside seemed to take the opportunity of becoming more luxuriant than usual. A few rough trunks lying against the tufts of fern and a quiet donkey made the bit perfect as a foreground, and close behind it rose a steep hill half orchard and half grass. The first time we took this walk the primroses were still abundant, but they were beginning to be eclipsed by the other flowers of the hedgerow. As we advanced along this lane chatting happily and gathering flowers we could see before us the overlapping hills covered by the Chambercombe woods.

The image created is one of a contented and happy couple enjoying the opportunity to be together, and who, moreover, were able to chat in a relaxed and open fashion, unburdened by prying eyes.

The Leweses also spent time in the evening being entertained in the company of fellow travellers. Mrs Webster and her daughter Miss Webster had taken rooms in the same villa, and along with George Eliot and Lewes, they sometimes made up a foursome and passed the evening enjoying conversation and musical interludes. They had also made the acquaintance of Mr Tugwell, a local curate and a collector of anemones. He was therefore someone Lewes was particularly keen to get to know. In her journal, George Eliot recalls the following:

Mr Tugwell's acquaintance was a real acquisition to us, not only because he was a companion and helper in zoological pursuits, but because to know him was to know of another sweet nature in the world. It is always good to know, if only in passing, a charming human being – it refreshes one like flowers, and woods and clear brooks. One Sunday evening we walked up to his pretty house to carry back some proofs of his, and he induced us to go in and have coffee with him. He played on his Harmonium and we chatted pleasantly. The last evening of our stay at Ilfracombe he came to see us in Mrs Webster's drawing-room, and we had music until nearly 11 o'clock. A pleasant recollection.

Tenby

On 26 June, the Leweses' holiday in Ilfracombe came to an end. Before returning home, they were to stay in Tenby, West Wales, for a short break, and this involved a three-hour wait at Swansea railway station. Although George Eliot described Swansea as looking 'dismal' and as smelling 'detestably', the wait also provided her with the opportunity to spot two cockle women and the chance to write an impressive piece of description:

> One of them was the grandest woman I ever saw – six feet high, carrying herself like a Greek Warrior, and treading the earth with unconscious majesty. They wore large woollen shawls of a rich brown, doubled lengthwise, with the end thrown back again over the left shoulder, so as to fall behind in graceful folds. The grander of the two carried a great pitcher in her hand, and wore a quaint little bonnet set upright on her head. Her face was weather beaten and wizened, but her eyes were bright and piercing and the lines of her face, with its high cheek-bones, strong and characteristic. The other carried her pitcher on her head, and was also a fine old woman, but less majestic in her port than her companion. The guard at the railway told us that one of the porters had been insolent the other day to a cockle woman, and that she immediately pitched him off the platform into the road below!

George Eliot enjoyed including such pieces of description in her journal and had been considering writing fiction for quite some time. Lewes had also been prodding her to do so, partly because he recognised her skill and partly because he realised there was more money to be made from novel-writing than article-writing. She continued to contemplate such a venture throughout her Tenby holiday, recalling:

> But one morning as I was lying in bed, thinking what should be the subject of my first story, my thoughts merged themselves into a dreamy doze, and I imagined myself writing a story of which the title was – 'The Sad Fortunes of the Reverend Amos Barton'. I was soon wide awake again and told G. He said, 'O what a capital title!' and from that time I had settled in my mind that this should be my first story. George used to say, 'It may be a failure – it may be that you are unable to write fiction. Or perhaps it may be just good enough to warrant you trying again...' But his prevalent impression was that though I could hardly write a poor novel, my effort would want the highest quality of fiction – dramatic presentation. He used to say, 'You have wit, description and philosophy – those go a good way towards the production of a novel. It is worthwhile for you to try the experiment.'

However, deciding to start a career as a novelist and actually being able to begin proved to be two entirely different issues for George Eliot. As soon as she and Lewes returned home to Richmond, Lewes departed once more – this time to take his sons to Switzerland. Left alone and with only the prospect of work for the *Westminster Review* to comfort her, George Eliot fell ill with toothache. Although still in agony once the tooth was removed, John Chapman insisted her articles for the journal were completed, *Silly Novels by Lady Novelists* being one of them.

On 23 September George Eliot finally wrote in her journal:

> Began to write "The Sad Fortunes of the Reverend Amos Barton" which I hope to make one of a series called "Scenes of Clerical Life".

On Monday, 2 October, her journal contains the following entry:

> I have brought my story to the end of the second chapter.

By the end of October, she had begun the fifth chapter of her story and by Wednesday, 5 November, it had finally been completed. Lewes was impressed with what she had written. Indeed, so much so that he became, in effect, her literary agent, and decided he would be the one to send out her manuscript on her behalf. In choosing John Blackwood as the recipient of her work, Lewes made an excellent choice.

John Blackwood

John Blackwood was the sixth son of William Blackwood, head of Blackwood's publishing company and also of the extremely popular *Blackwood's Magazine*. In 1845, following the death of his eldest brother, John Blackwood became the editor of the magazine, and in 1852, following the death of another brother, he also became head of the publishing business. He was renowned for being a patient and giving editor, someone who was willing to spend time offering suggestions to a writer in order to ensure their work was as polished as possible. He was particularly keen when he received George Eliot's manuscript, which Lewes had sent anonymously, claiming it to be the work of a shy friend with clerical connections. During the years he published her novels, Blackwood realised that he had before him not just the work of an extremely capable writer, but possibly the writings of a genius. His excellence as a publisher was highlighted by the fact that throughout their publishing relationship, which lasted for all of Blackwood's life until his death in 1879, any notes he had to give and any suggestions he had to make were always done with the best of intentions, and never came across as too critical or judgemental. This was particularly useful to George Eliot: as someone who always took on board criticism before appreciating positive comments, it meant that her confidence was not overly shaken. However, Blackwood did indeed have some doubts about *Scenes of Clerical Life* when he received the first story. He worried that it might be too religious or even appear to mock the clergy. Usually he would ask to see a new writer's whole manuscript before accepting it but on this occasion, due to some persuasive words from Lewes, he agreed to accept *Scenes of Clerical Life* on the basis of the first story alone.

Fiction in print

On New Year's Day 1857, the first instalment of *The Sad Fortunes of the Reverend Amos Barton* appeared in *Blackwood's Magazine*. *Mr Gilfil's Love-Story* appeared in instalments throughout the spring of the same year and *Janet's Repentance* was published between July and November. By this time, George Eliot had written to John Blackwood and told him the name of his new author. A story would later emerge that she had chosen the name George because it was Lewes's Christian name and Eliot because it was easily pronounceable. Speculation remained about whether Blackwood, among others, eventually guessed that Lewes's shy friend was indeed his partner, but if they believed so, her publishers in particular preferred to remain tight-lipped about it. It was their belief that no good could come from their potential readership knowing that one of their newest writers carried even a hint of scandal along with her. It could impact heavily upon sales, their reputation as a publishing company and furthermore, it could end George Eliot's career as a novelist before it had even begun. But in reality, the subterfuge was probably nothing more than a game that was being played by both sides. It suited the Leweses and John Blackwood to pretend that George Eliot truly was George Lewes's close male friend. Any money owed to George Eliot was paid in the form of a cheque to Lewes, who apparently dealt with all of his friend's banking matters. It wasn't until John Blackwood actually visited the Leweses at home that Blackwood was forced to acknowledge that he had known for quite some time about George Eliot's true identity, and he had already guessed the real identity of the writer whose work he had published.

Response of Dickens

In January 1858, *Scenes of Clerical Life* was published as a two-volume novel. Presentation copies were sent to among others, Charles Dickens, William Makepeace Thackeray and Mrs Carlyle, all of whom wrote letters of thanks. In his letter, Dickens hints that certain aspects of the volume led him to believe its author was a woman:

Chapter Ten

My Dear Sir,   January 18ᵗʰ 1858

I have been so strongly affected by the two first tales in the book you have had the kindness to send me through Messrs. Blackwood, that I hope you will excuse my writing to you to express my admiration of their extraordinary merit. The exquisite truth and delicacy, both of the humour and the pathos of those stories, I have never seen the like of; and they have impressed me in a manner that I should find it very difficult to describe to you, if I had the impertinence to try.

In addressing these few words to the creator of the sad fortunes of Mr Amos Barton, and the sad love story of Mr Gilfil, I am (I presume) bound to adopt the name that it pleases the excellent writer to assume. I can suggest no better one; but I should have been strongly disposed, if I had been left to my own devices, to address the said writer as a woman. I have observed what seems to me to be such womanly touches, in those moving fictions, that the assurance on the title-page is insufficient to satisfy me, even now. If they originated with no woman, I believe that no man ever before had the art of making himself, mentally, so like a woman since the world began.

You will not suppose that I have any vulgar wish to fathom your secret. I mention the point as one of great interest to me – not of mere curiosity. If it should ever suit your convenience and inclination, to show me the face of the man or the woman who has written so charmingly, it will be a very memorable occasion to me. If otherwise, I shall always hold that impalpable personage in loving attachment and respect, and shall yield myself up to all future utterances from the same source, with a confidence in their making me wiser and better.

Your obliged and faithful servant and admirer,
Charles Dickens.

Dickens is certainly fulsome in his praise here, particularly for the first two stories in the collection. He also finds it hard to believe that

Scenes of Clerical Life could possibly have been written by a man, and it causes the reader to speculate as to how far he might have guessed the true identity of George Eliot. Certainly, by the time she published *Adam Bede*, he knew she was a woman and began his letter of appreciation with, *My Dear Madam*.

Isaac Evans

Life for the Leweses was certainly looking more promising than it had done previously. George Lewes was gradually beginning to mention to his sons that he had a special friend who would like to be able to treat them to small gifts, with the hope that one day they could all meet as a family. George Eliot had experienced success with her first publication and was beginning to consider a second work entitled *Adam Bede*. However, one problem still caused her pain: her lack of ability to share all her good news with the Evans family. She had tried to communicate with her brother Isaac in the previous year, realising that she needed to tell him about a change in her circumstances. She and Lewes had been holidaying in Jersey at the time, and perhaps feeling relaxed and comfortable, she decided it would be an ideal time to write to him:

> My Dear Brother,
> You will be surprised, I dare say, but I hope not sorry, to hear that I have changed my name, and have someone to take care of me in the world. The event is not a sudden one, though it may appear sudden in its announcement to you. My husband has been known to me for several years, and I am well acquainted with his mind and character. He is occupied entirely with scientific and learned pursuits, is several years older than myself, and has three boys, two of whom are at school in Switzerland, and one in England.

After reading this letter it becomes obvious that George Eliot was particularly careful about the phrasing she used when informing Isaac of her relationship. The actual news is carefully presented, and she is insistent that she and Lewes are actually married and therefore is keen to point out she has formally taken her husband's surname. This could either be to spare Isaac embarrassment and pain, or because she truly believed she and Lewes were married in every single sense, except legally. Later in the letter she also shows concern for her sister Chrissey's health, and asks for a sum of money to be paid to her. Regardless, Isaac was so infuriated by her news that he refused to reply personally. Instead, the matter was referred to his solicitor, Vincent Holbeche, who replied on his behalf:

Dear Mrs Lewes,   9th June 1857

I have had an interview with your brother in consequence of your letter to him announcing your marriage. He is so much hurt at your not having previously made some communication to him as to your intention and prospects that he cannot make up his mind to write, feeling that he could not do so in a brotherly spirit. I have at his request undertaken to address you in the belief that you will receive my letter as coming from an old friend of the family. Your brother and sister (who is gradually gaining a little strength) are naturally anxious to obtain some information respecting your altered state. Perhaps you will not object to make some communication to me which I may convey to them. Permit me to ask when and where you were married and what is the occupation of Mr Lewes, who I think you refer to in your letter as being actively employed, and where his residence is as you request a remittance to be made to his bankers in London by the Trustees under your Father's Will. I shall be happy to hear from you and trust the result of your communication may be that of your brother corresponding directly with you, and remain, Dear Mrs Lewes,

Yours very faithfully,
Vincent Holbeche.

Isaac's instruction, through his solicitor, to have more details about his sister's wedding poses the suggestion that he was already beginning to suspect all was not as it seemed from her correspondence. He was also angry that his position as head of the Evans family had been compromised through his sister's lack of communication. In his eyes, and according to mid-nineteenth century patriarchal belief, she should have at least done him the courtesy of writing to inform him of the flowering of her friendship with Lewes, and asked for her brother's advice, even if she had no intention of listening to it. If he felt snubbed, his anger might be understood. Isaac was after all a traditionalist, and someone who believed the conventions of society should be strictly adhered to. If he was beginning to believe the true state of affairs, and that there was no actual marriage, his anger would be palpable. George Eliot was forced to confess the true nature of her married state in the letter she sent to her brother's solicitor by return:

My Dear Sir,   June 13th 1857
I have just received your letter written to me by my brother's request, and I willingly reply to it at once by a statement of the facts concerning which you desire information; the more so, because I anticipated the probability of my having to correspond with you as a joint Trustee under my Father's Will.

My brother has judged wisely in begging you to communicate with me. If his feelings towards me are unfriendly, there is no necessity for his paining himself by any direct intercourse with me; indeed, if he had written to me in a tone which I could not recognise (since I am not conscious of having done him any injury) I must myself have employed a third person as a correspondent.

Mr Lewes is a well-known writer, author among other things of the 'Life of Goethe' and the 'Biographical History of Philosophy'. Our marriage is not a legal one, though it is regarded by us both as a sacred bond. He is unable at present to contract a legal marriage, because, though long deprived of his first wife by her misconduct, he is not legally divorced.

I have been his wife and have borne his name for three years: a fact which has been known to all my personal friends except the members of my own family, from whom I have withheld it, because knowing that their view of life differ in many respects from my own, I wished not to give them unnecessary pain. Other considerations, however, have at length determined me to inform them of my circumstances and of the responsibilities for life, which I have undertaken.

It may be desirable to mention to you that I am not dependant on anyone, the larger part of my income for several years having been derived from my own constant labour as a writer. You will perceive, therefore, that in my conduct towards my own family I have not been guided by any motives of self-interest, since I have been neither in the reception, nor the expectation of the slightest favour from them.

It was certainly brave of George Eliot to prevaricate no longer, and to tell her brother, in simple terms, of the true legal status of her relationship with Lewes and of his actual marital status with another woman. It is also possible to tell from the tone of this letter how clearly she wants to communicate her own independence, and how her reasons for writing to Isaac had nothing to do with money, and everything to do with wishing to inform her family of the changes in her life. Isaac, however, refused to buckle, and was not at all moved emotionally by his sister's story. Not only would he cut off all contact with her until after Lewes's death, when she legally married John Cross, but he also absolutely refused to allow anyone else in the family to communicate with her either. She was to be ostracised from them completely, something which remained a source of great pain to her.

Adam Bede

In spite of any personal pain felt by George Eliot, her writing life began to flourish. After the success of *Scenes of Clerical Life,* she was keen to start on her second piece, this time a novel set in the countryside at the very end of the eighteenth century. She worked on *Adam Bede* throughout most of 1858, including during the three months spent in Munich with Lewes, where their travels also took them to Salzburg, Vienna, Prague and Dresden. The novel was published at the start of the following year and received immediate success. Readers were particularly drawn to the beautiful descriptions of the English countryside George Eliot had included in her book, especially when Hetty Sorrel, desperate and alone, is looking for sanctuary from her problems:

> It was about ten o'clock when Hetty set off, and the slight hoar frost that had whitened the hedges in the early morning had disappeared as the sun mounted the cloudless sky. Bright February days have a stronger charm of hope about

them than any other days in the year. One likes to pause
in the mild rays of the sun, and look over the gates at the
patient plough-horses turning at the end of the furrow, and
think that the beautiful year is all before one. The birds seem
to feel just the same: their notes are as clear as the clear air.
There are no leaves on the trees and hedgerows, but how
green all the grassy fields are! and the dark purplish brown
of the ploughed earth and of the bare branches is beautiful
too. What a glad world this looks like, as one drives or rides
along the valleys and over the hills!

(Chapter Thirty-Five, *Adam Bede*)

George Eliot's descriptions, however, were intended to do more than simply
provide the reader with something beautiful to read, or a means by which
they could easily conjure in their mind the world she had created. Her
descriptions of the countryside were meant to act as a foil for the characters
who were placed firmly at the centre of them. Although the February
morning Hetty is experiencing is one of beauty, she is going through one
of the worst times of her life and facing abandonment by the father of the
baby she is carrying. Similarly, although the surrounding countryside is
beautiful, as is Hetty in a superficial way, beneath her charm and attractive
features she is selfish and self-absorbed. George Eliot is posing a question
to her readers about the significance of inner and outer realities, and how
the two do not always match. It is up to the individual to try to make sense
of the world around them and try to differentiate between the reality of the
inner and outer world they are regularly faced with.

Adam Bede is a man with many qualities and in these he is similar to
Robert Evans – certain to be noticed and rewarded for his dedication and
hard work, even by those who are socially superior to him. His downfall,
however, is that he is blinded by his own prejudices and beliefs. For
example, Hetty's attractive features blind him to the fact that she is
capable of wrongdoing, his father's drinking hardens him to any other
aspects of his character, and it is only when he has experienced his
father's death, Hetty's misfortune and feelings for Dinah, that he softens
in his approach to others. Robert Evans could also be a man blinded by
his own prejudice. He found it hard to forgive his daughter's change in
religious beliefs, and this was surely something else she had in mind
when creating the character of Adam.

Reviews

Many of the contemporary reviews of *Adam Bede* were positive, some were glowing. Others, such as the one posted in the *Daily News* in February 1859, were a little more mixed:

> It is too often a mere banal phrase in newspaper criticism to say of a work that it is not an ordinary one, most assuredly, without any banality, we can say as much of the work before us. It is not open to the praise or accusation belonging to the most modern works of fiction – that it has attained a respectable mediocrity. Its merits are of the highest order on the one hand, while on the other it has great and grievous defects. The author will never belong to that class of pregnant writers who furnish year after year a series of decently written volumes, which take their places for a time on the shelves of circulating libraries, get reviewed in newspapers, are talked about in literary circles, and then sink into oblivion. Mr Eliot, or whoever the real author of this work may be, will either write little more, or take his stand among the first writers of the age. But to effect this, he will either have to correct many serious errors in the conception of his narratives, and what is still more difficult, in his own appreciation of the sympathies and feelings of the world.
>
> Hitherto he has shown a great – we might almost say an utter – want of invention. Nothing could be more meagre than the plots of his former work. The plot of the present is as commonplace as possible. We have two heroes and two heroines. Of the heroes, one is a stalwart carpenter – full of right notions, with no faults except that of an overstrained standard of principles, which causes him to judge others too harshly; the other a young country squire – handsome, gay, full of good intentions, anxious to make everyone happy but without sufficient steadiness…
>
> But we have a yet more serious objection to urge than mere poverty of plot. The sympathies which the author evokes are altogether contrary to his own intention and to the moral of his tale…

The critic continues by commenting that the writer has inadvertently created more sympathy for Hetty than he intended, and that the reader therefore feels more sympathy for her in the final stages of the novel than any other character, in spite of what she has done, However, the review ends on a positive note with the critic concluding that the writer has the potential to take 'his place amongst the best writers of fiction which the age can boast'. Indeed, even though the critic picks up on some weaknesses with the plot of *Adam Bede,* they have also been quite perceptive. For example, they too have doubts about the author of the novel, wondering if it really is a man called George Eliot. They also consider the possibility of a long-term future for the author, and genuinely believe they have an opportunity to become one of the best.

Much to the consternation of George Eliot and Lewes, the argument about the real name and gender of the writer of *Scenes of Clerical Life* and *Adam Bede* was still rumbling on and threatening to overshadow any achievements her novels were garnering. Herbert Spencer had already been told the truth, and apparently, he found it hard to lie when asked bluntly what he knew, which led to John Chapman also guessing correctly the true identity of the writer of *Adam Bede*. Gradually, of course, news of George Eliot's real identity spread, and this, coupled with her unusual relationship with Lewes, gave some readers pause for thought, especially when the knowledge passed from London and into the provinces. Some angry readers at the time believed they had been forced to digest lessons on morality from a writer who was living an immoral life, and even worse, a female writer who was posing as a man.

Double standards

This sense of hysteria against women was reflected in the behaviour displayed towards the couple. While Lewes was generally free to go into the city and take advantage of its cultural and dining experiences, either alone or with friends, without real fear of recrimination, such opportunities were firmly closed to George Eliot. She would certainly face reprisal and snubs if she risked going to many public events, and while this gave her the opportunity to write without disturbance, it also highlighted society's hypocrisy and double standards towards women who had supposedly fallen from their moral pedestal.

Chapter Ten

George Eliot was already planning her next novel, *The Mill on the Floss,* when she and Lewes moved to Holly Lodge, Wimbledon Road, Wandsworth. In between she wrote a ghost story, *The Lifted Veil,* and took a holiday with Lewes to North Wales. The holiday was blighted by the number of other tourists also hoping to enjoy a break from the everyday rush of city life. The trip did allow them, however, to make a visit to see Chrissey's daughters at Lichfield before their return to London. Chrissey had defied Isaac's rule and contacted her sister the previous year, eager to hear news from the sister to whom she had once been so close. Chrissey had died from consumption in March 1859 and visiting her nieces was the nearest George Eliot would ever come to being able to see her sister again.

Chapter Eleven

In which George Eliot becomes a mother figure to three sons, and introduces *The Mill on the Floss* and *Silas Marner* to the world

All the deepest fibres of the mother's memory were stirred, and the young man whose voice took a gentler tone when he spoke to her, was one with the babe she had loved, with a love new to her, before he was born.

(*Middlemarch*)

When Agnes Jervis Lewes and George Lewes initially separated, their three sons, Charles, Thornie and Bertie were aged 12, 10 and 8 respectively. Too young to be told anything about their mother's affair, they had no real knowledge of why their parents had separated, knowing only that they no longer lived together. By 1857 all three boys were being educated in a school in Bern, Switzerland, and so it was relatively easy to ensure they were kept safely hidden from any hint of scandal caused by their father's relationship with George Eliot. If ever the couple were near Bern during their travels, Lewes would visit his sons alone, meaning that they were all still unaware of their father's new situation.

It is difficult to know why things changed, but by the summer of 1859 Lewes felt ready to tell his sons the truth about the 'friend' he had previously mentioned and who had sent gifts and treats. He explained as gently as he could about their mother's infidelity and moved on swiftly, telling them about his new relationship with someone who made him extremely happy. All three sons took the news well, and the following year, when Lewes was due to make his next visit, he took George Eliot with him. By all accounts the meeting was a successful one, and the boys came up with a number of names for their new 'mother', including, 'Mater', 'Mutter', 'Mutterchen' and 'Little Mother'. Even more change was brought into the Leweses' family life because eldest son Charles returned with them to England, where he lived at Holly Lodge and sat the Post Office exam. He was followed by Thornie in September, in readiness for his move to Edinburgh and preparation for the East Indian Service and three years later, in 1863, by Bertie, who was to be trained in farming. In a letter to Charles Bray on 18 July 1860, it is easy to see how quickly Lewes's sons became an integral part of George Eliot's life, and to note that she was fully supportive of suspending her own plans with Lewes regarding a house move in order to ensure the boys' needs were fully catered for:

> We are quite uncertain about our plans at present. Our second boy, Thornie, is going to leave Hofwyl and be placed in some more expensive position, in order to the carrying on of his education in a more complete way, so that we are thinking of avoiding for the present any final establishment of ourselves, which would necessarily be attended with additional outlay. Besides these material cares draw rather too severely on my strength and spirits. But until Charlie's career has taken shape, we frame no definite projects.

The Mill on the Floss

Throughout 1859, George Eliot had also been kept busy with the planning and writing of *The Mill on the Floss,* ready for its publication date in the spring of 1860. The couple were holidaying in Italy at the time and this is something they were soon to make a habit of, as George Eliot preferred to be out of the country when members of the reading public were first allowed a glimpse of her work. She still found the initial response to her novels caused her worry and concern, as she tended to focus on any negative comments that appeared among the many favourable reviews. The other problem George Eliot was going to face was that out of those who knew her true identity, there would always be critics who judged her apparent lack of morals instead of her actual written work.

Sales of *The Mill on the Floss* were positive, 6,000 copies sold in under two months, but the reviews were somewhat mixed. The critic of the *Saturday Review* wrote:

> Currer Bell and George Eliot, and we may add George Sand, all like to dwell on love as a strange overmastering force… But we are not quite sure that it is quite consistent with feminine delicacy to lay so much stress on the bodily feelings of the other sex…because they occur it does not follow that spiritual doubts and conflicts are a proper subject for a novelist.

It very much seems as if this critic had a particular loathing of any reading material aimed at women, and considering he (presumably!) seems to feel ladies should not come into contact with any novels which touch upon the themes of love, spiritual doubts and conflict, it is difficult to conceive of reading matter for the opposite sex which he would deem to be appropriate.

The inability to accept George Eliot because of her relationship choices has long since failed to prejudice readers against her novels, especially *The Mill on the Floss*. Where once reviewers were shocked by Maggie's temptation to be with Stephen Guest, readers now appreciate her depiction as an intelligent, passionate woman who was afraid that her gender and lack of an expansive education had led to her missing out on all of the many exciting ventures life had to offer.

George Eliot remained thankfully undeterred by the negative reviews, perhaps realising for once that many were tainted less by a dislike of her writing, than by a dislike of her personal situation, or by a preconceived notion of what ideas and themes novels should contain. While sales remained so positive, and with Lewes's support, she would continue to write her novels. On 12 June 1861, she wrote the following to her publisher, John Blackwood:

> I am writing a story which came across my other plans by a sudden inspiration. I don't know at present whether it will resolve itself into a book short enough for me to complete before Easter, or whether it will expand beyond that possibility. It seems to me that nobody will take any interest

in it but myself, for it is extremely unlike the popular stories going; but Mr Lewes declares that I am wrong and says it is as good as anything that I have done. It is a story of old-fashioned village life, which has unfolded itself from the merest millet-seed of thought. I think I get slower and more timid in my writing, but perhaps worry about houses and servants and boys, with want of bodily strength may have something to do with that. I hope to be quiet now.

It has continued to be one of the conundrums of George Eliot's life that while living such an unconventional life, she often succumbed to the typical concerns of a housewife, and worried about servants and family life – the sort of problems Mrs Beeton gave such sound advice about in her *Book of Household Management.* George Eliot never remonstrated with women who wished to spend their lives concerned with such matters; she only wanted them to have the freedom to do so with a husband of their choice, and with one who treated them with love and respect.

Silas Marner

The novel George Eliot was referring to in her letter to Blackwood was *Silas Marner,* which was published at the beginning of April 1861. Her tale of small community life just before the outbreak of the Industrial Revolution focused on the eponymous protagonist, his role as a solitary weaver, and the religious and personal epiphany he undergoes when a young child toddles into his cottage. The reviews were almost all not only positive, but glowing. In a letter to Sara Hennell, dated 18 April 1861, George Eliot recorded her feelings regarding the response to her latest publication:

> I am very much cheered by the way in which "Silas" is received. I hope it has made some slight pleasure for you too...

But of course, George Eliot, in spite of her sometimes fragile health, her migraines and her aches and pains, was already busy planning and writing her next novel.

Chapter Twelve

In which George Eliot writes two more novels, moves house and suffers further tragedy

Our dead are never dead to us until we have forgotten them: they can be injured by us, they can be wounded; they know all our penitence, all our aching sense that their place is empty, all the kisses we bestow on the smallest relic of their presence.

(*Adam Bede*)

George Eliot and Lewes had been in Florence, Italy, when *Silas Marner* was published and typically, research was already underway for her next novel, *Romola*. The holiday included plenty of trips to the Magliabecchian Library and opportunities to study the landscape, architecture and people of the city in which the novel was to be set. The Leweses were also fortunate to have Thomas Trollope, the novelist Anthony Trollope's brother, as a guide to Florence, the city he had chosen to make his home.

Upon her arrival home, however, George Eliot found herself stumbling with the novel and was alarmed to discover that writing her manuscript did not come easily, regardless of the amount of research she had completed. This was the first and indeed only one of her novels to take place outside of Britain, and this, coupled with the fact that it was set in the fifteenth century, made dialogue and speech patterns particularly difficult to emulate. It was certainly the most ambitious of her novels in terms of historical accuracy and plot, set as it was at a turbulent time of Florentine history, with the banishment of the Medici family and the rise of the religious zealot Savonarola. At the heart of the novel is Romola, beautiful and intellectual, a carer for her blind father, the scholar Bardo de' Bardi, and married to Tito, a man in whom she ultimately loses faith.

Romola's beauty is made obvious to the reader from the moment she is first introduced to the reader:

> The only spot of bright colour in the room was made by the hair of a tall maiden of seventeen or eighteen, who was standing before a carved leggio, or reading-desk, such as is often seen in the choirs of Italian churches. The hair was of a reddish gold colour, enriched by an unbroken small ripple, such as may be seen in the sunset clouds on grandest autumnal evenings. It was confined by a black fillet above her small ears, from which it rippled forward again, and made a natural veil for her neck above her square-cut gown of black rascia, or serge. Her eyes were bent on a large volume placed before her; one long white hand rested on the reading-desk, and the other clasped the back of her father's chair.
>
> (Book One, Chapter Five, *Romola*)

Romola's beauty is combined with intelligence and this, coupled with her youth, seems to make her an ideal predecessor for Dorothea, whose youth also encourages her to make a less-than-successful marriage.

In spite of finding Romola more difficult to write than her other novels, George Eliot was finally able to write the following in her journal on 9 June 1863:

> Put the last stroke to "Romola" Ebenezer! Went in the evening to La Gazza Ladra. The manuscript of "Romola" bears the following inscription:
>
> To the Husband whose perfect love has been the best source of her insight and strength, this manuscript is given by his devoted wife, the writer.

A new publisher

Lewes was always ready to give George Eliot all the praise and support she needed, but this time he had also gone one step further and had found her another publisher. Unlike her other novels, *Romola* was not to be published by John Blackwood, but by George Smith of Smith,

Elder and Co., who had been eager to publish one of George Eliot's manuscripts for quite some time. In her letter informing Blackwood of this latest development, George Eliot told him Smith's offer had been especially handsome. In fact, he had also offered work to Lewes as chief literary advisor, and suggested he publish some of his natural history articles which had originally appeared in *The Cornhill Magazine* (a publication which was owned by Smith, Elder and Co.) as a book. He also offered £10,000 to George Eliot for the entire copyright of *Romola*, an incredibly substantial sum at the time (equal to just over £1 million in 2020). Blackwood was magnificently courteous in his response, secretly believing that Lewes was behind the whole decision. However, Blackwood did get some small revenge when he discovered that George Eliot was only willing to accept £7,000 for *Romola* (equal to £838,000 in 2020). The £10,000 was a prerequisite of her novel becoming longer and being written in sixteen instalments, which she refused. Money was never a motivating factor for George Eliot, particularly when it came to compromising her art.

Romola

Romola was first published in serial form, and although some reviews did appear, most critics waited for the publication of the work in novel form before making any comment. Generally, the response was positive: many readers had now begun to see George Eliot as a writer with messages to teach, and whether they agreed with them or not, her writing style was believed to be something for which she should be commended.

As was usual, the Leweses had arranged to take a holiday as soon as work on George Eliot's latest novel was complete. This time, they visited the Isle of Wight, which in a letter to Sara Hennell, dated 21 June 1863, she compared to Jersey:

> This place is perfect, reminding me of Jersey, in its combination of luxuriant greenth with the delights of a sandy beach. At the end of our week, if the weather is warmer, we shall go on to Freshwater for our remaining few days. But the wind at present is a little colder than one desires it, when the object is to get rid of a cough, and unless

it gets milder we shall go back to Shanklin. I am enjoying
the hedge-row grasses and flowers with something like a
released prisoner's feeling – it is so long since I had a bit of
real English country.

In spite of the cold and suffering from a cough, the real emotions
underlying George Eliot's words are surely contentment and happiness.
This joy was to be continued after the Leweses arrived home as they
were in the middle of purchasing a house together. It was the first time
they had actually owned a home, as previously they had lodged in rooms
or rented houses. This was to be an exciting time in their lives, and
perhaps allowed George Eliot to experience what so many brides before
her had always had the chance to look forward to, but which hitherto
she had been forbidden from anticipating: the opportunity to furnish
and decorate a home of her own. The Priory, North Bank, situated in St
John's Wood, was a graceful house with gabled windows and a turret
effect. Steps from the door led into a pretty garden and the rooms were
expansive and well-decorated. The couple were unable to move into the
Priory until November 1863, and by 14 November, George Eliot was
able to write the following in her journal:

> We are now nearly in order, only wanting a few details of
> furniture to finish our equipment for a new stage in our life's
> journey.

However, she was obviously keen to move onto other ventures, her
concern with decorating having been short-lived:

> I long very much to have done thinking of upholstery, and
> to get again a consciousness that there are better things than
> that to reconcile one with life.

Felix Holt

It was not until March 1865 that George Eliot finally felt able to write
her next novel. Bouts of severe ill health suffered by Lewes as well as
herself, and an abortive attempt at playwriting had all taken their toll,

and so *Felix Holt: The Radical* was not started until almost a year and a half had passed. All in all, her novel about a young Radical and the political beliefs that shaped his life took a great deal of research, particularly concerning the legal aspects of inheritance clauses. Set in the fictitious Treby at the time of the First Reform Act (1832), Harold Transome defies his traditionally Tory family by standing as a Radical in the local elections. At the same time, Felix Holt, himself a Radical, becomes friends with a dissenting minister, but is unsure how to treat Esther, the minister's beautiful but vain stepdaughter. The plot is further developed when it is discovered that Harold Transome's electioneering agent, Matthew Jermyn, has been embezzling money. However, it is Esther's character who undergoes the most life-altering change, as she is forced, through circumstance, to recognise what is truly important in life. In a letter to Mrs Bray on 5 June 1866, George Eliot commemorated the completion of her manuscript by writing:

> I finished writing Felix Holt on the last day of May, after days and nights of throbbing and palpitation – chiefly, I suppose, from a nervous excitement which I was not strong enough to support well. As soon as I had done I felt better, and have been a new creature ever since, though a little overdone with visits from friends and attention (miserabile dictu!) to petticoats etc.

Felix Holt was to be published by John Blackwood, George Smith having turned it down when Lewes revealed his asking price for the copyright was £5,000 (equal to almost £600,000 in 2020). In spite of being ignored when it came to publishing *Romola,* Blackwood was keen to publish a writer of George Eliot's calibre once again, and so he was willing to overlook any past offence Lewes may have caused him. Indeed, he was to remain George Eliot's publisher for the rest of her writing career.

Felix Holt was published in the early summer of 1866, and as was their habit, the Leweses were travelling through Holland, Belgium and Germany when the book was released. The novel was a success with most critics, although less so with its wider readership, and indeed, it lost Blackwood money. The anonymous critic of the *Saturday Review,* wrote on 16 June 1866:

The opening lines of Felix Holt affect the reader like the first notes of the prelude to an old familiar melody. We find ourselves once more among the Midland homesteads, the hedgerows, "liberal homes of unmarketable beauty", and the great corn-stacks in the rick-yard, while here too, as in the old Loamshire of Adam Bede, "the busy scenes of the shuttle and the wheels of the roaring furnace of the shaft and the pulley" lie "in the midst of the large-spaced, slow-moving life of homesteads and far-away cottages and oak-sheltered parks."

It seems, argues the critic, that readers enjoy George Eliot's depiction of typical, English country life. The reviewer concludes with the following praise:

> Of her exquisite humour, her subtlety and delicacy of analysis, the wide suggestiveness of her bits of "aside", and her style which is so fascinating because it is so exact an outward expression of the deep and mellow power with which her mind works and by which it is coloured – of all these we need not speak. They are as perfect and as delightful as they ever were.

Praise indeed! Some reviewers, however, criticised her inability to add poetic charm to her prose, and George Eliot, ever mindful of those who found fault with her work, decided to spend time focusing on the creation of verse in order to help boost the 'charm' of her descriptive passages. For the next year or so, she focused almost entirely on the writing of poetry – a holiday to Spain helped with the writing of *The Spanish Gypsy*, which transpired to be the longest of her poems. At its heart is the character of Fedalma, a young woman living in fifteenth-century Andalucía, who finds herself caught between the demands of two entirely different worlds and duties, resulting in a change to be made between a life following her heritage as a gypsy, or a life of luxury with her fiancé Don Silva. Reviews for the poem were mixed, but George Eliot continued to write poetry, including the autobiographical *Brother and Sister,* and it was not until 1869 that she began work on her next novel.

While life at the Priory had been busy, Lewes's sons had been forging careers for themselves. Charles had settled down admirably well to his job with the Post Office and his father and 'mater' had found him lodgings at 10 Harewood Square in order to make his commute to the city as easy as possible. Bertie, who was perhaps the least intelligent of the three sons, was hugely looking forward to a life spent farming the land and was enjoying the experience of learning how to become a successful farmer in the countryside around Stratford-upon-Avon. It was Thornie, the middle son, who was causing the Leweses most concern. His training in Edinburgh for the East Indian Service was not going particularly well, and ultimately ended with him failing his final exams. He next decided that the life of a soldier would suit him best, and revealed plans to go and fight the Russians in Poland. This left both Lewes and George Eliot extremely concerned, but help came in the form of close family friend, Barbara Leigh Smith Bodichon. She persuaded Thornie that he could still have a life of adventure if he travelled to South Africa and tried his hand at big game shooting in Natal. Thornie believed this to be a splendid idea and left Britain in October 1863. The Leweses were both hugely relieved, and it appeared that danger had been averted. They were especially pleased when Bertie discovered his brother had obtained a grant to farm land in Natal, and so decided to join him.

However, worry was never far away where Thornie was concerned, and it took only two years before disturbing news started trickling through to Britain from South Africa. Thornie was suffering from constant back pain and losing a large amount of weight. Lewes sent money to his son and told him to come home immediately in order to receive attention from a doctor. It was almost six months before Thornie arrived home, looking wretched and alarmingly thin. Unable to sit on a chair due to the spasms of pain that racked his body, he simply lay down on the floor, waiting for the pain to ease. For the next six months he suffered, with very little relief from the agony that was making his life so miserable. His illness, likely to be tuberculosis of the spine, was mercifully a short one, and by October 1869 he was dead. Sadly, he was not to be the only one of Lewes's sons to be taken by tuberculosis. For a time, Bertie flourished in Natal, marrying and having two children. But by 1875 he too would be dead, killed by the same illness that took away his brother's life.

Chapter Thirteen

In which George Eliot writes her masterpiece, and suffers a greater tragedy than ever before

*That by desiring what is perfectly good, even when
we don't quite know what it is and cannot do what
we would, we are part of the divine power against
evil – widening the skirts of light and making the
struggle with darkness narrower.*

(*Middlemarch*)

Since the publication of *Felix Holt*, George Eliot had been focusing predominantly on writing poetry, but at the same time she had still been contemplating prospective ideas for her next novel, and the plot of *Middlemarch* was one she had been entertaining for quite some time. She began writing sections of Part Two throughout 1870, then put it aside to begin work on a short story called *Miss Brooke*. It was then that she realised the two pieces would work well together and began to weave them into one, recognising that Dorothea Brooke was destined to play an integral and unifying role.

Middlemarch, with its themes of societal expectations, marital imperfections and the role played by fate in the life of an individual determined to achieve, has successfully transcended time because it speaks to all generations throughout the decades. The characters in George Eliot's novel, to a lesser or greater degree, all experience the way in which society is necessary but restrictive: something all humans have to realise if they are to live a useful life. As a writer, George Eliot wished to warn her readers that none of us live in isolation. What we do as individuals impacts on others, and we must be mindful of this if we are to live alongside others in our community. Dr Lydgate, for example, has great plans as a doctor, but his marriage to Rosamond Vincy forces him into a world of conventionality, where money is more important than the research he wishes to undertake. Therefore, he is forced to abandon his personal goals whilst losing his integrity, and society at large is without the benefit of the medical research he could have undertaken. But George Eliot's characters are complex, and Lydgate is also full of conceit: given the opportunity, he tends to belittle older doctors in the community whose ideas he considers to be out of touch with new medical practices:

> Lydgate's conceit was of the arrogant sort, never simpering, never impertinent, but massive in its claims and benevolently contemptuous. He would do a great deal for noodles, being sorry for them, and feeling quite sure that they could have no power over him.
>
> (Book Two, Chapter Fifteen, *Middlemarch*)

The plot of *Middlemarch* has often been described as labyrinthine, but George Eliot cleverly ensured that all strands and characters were interwoven, so that one person's actions always impacted upon another, in however small a way. This reflection of real life in real communities drew readers to identify something of themselves in one or another of her creations, meaning that *Middlemarch* spoke to George Eliot's readers on many different levels.

Review

When the time came for the novel to be published, at Lewes's suggestion it was released in instalments as eight half-volumes. For such a huge novel, this seemed suitable. The first instalment appeared at the end of 1871 and the final one was published a year later. It appeared as one novel in 1873 and then again in 1874. From its very first run, it was considered to be a masterpiece. In his review for the *Spectator* on 7 December 1872, Richard Holt Hutton wrote:

> The whole tone of the story is so thoroughly noble, both morally and intellectually, that the care with which

George Eliot excludes all real faith in God from the religious side of her religious characters, conveys the same sort of shock with which, during the early days of eclipses, men must have seen the rays of light converging towards a centre of darkness. Mr Farebrother, – a favourite type with George Eliot, the rector in Adam Bede was another variety of him – Caleb Garth, the noble land agent and Dorothea, are all in the highest sense religious in temperament; two of them go through very keen temptations, and the struggles of one, Dorothea, are minutely and most powerfully described; but in all these cases, the province chosen for the religious temperament is solely the discharge of moral duty, and the side of these minds turned towards the divine centre of life, is conspicuous only by its absence, especially in Dorothea's case…Yes, say what we may, it is a great book.

Undoubtedly, *Middlemarch* finally established George Eliot as the highly regarded writer she had always aspired to be. Others believed it proved she had it within her to be a great moral teacher, but without the need to be overly preachy. *Middlemarch* also brought the Leweses wealth, fame, and some might add, for George Eliot at least, respectability. Throughout their relationship, Lewes had never suffered the same humiliations as his 'wife'. He had been able to socialise and visit people without fear of recrimination, while it was George Eliot who suffered at the hands of society's double standards. The publication of *Middlemarch* and its effusive reception, however, meant that respectability was now a tangible prospect, and people were hoping to be entertained by the writer of such a masterpiece at the Priory. Robert Browning was a regular visitor, as was Edward Burne-Jones and his wife, and George Eliot, a favourite writer of Queen Victoria, even met the royal princesses.

The Jewish religion

In spite of all this, both George Eliot's and Lewes's health continued to cause them problems. It was while they were visiting Homberg in central Germany, to take advantage of the fine air and waters, that George Eliot first conceived her idea for what would be her final novel,

Daniel Deronda. The novel centres around its eponymous protagonist who discovers he has Jewish heritage, so typically, George Eliot began reading as much as she could about the Jewish religion and its history. She began writing the novel as early as 1874, but made only slow progress at first. Continued ill health slowed her down. Lewes too was suffering and both of them hoped to take regular holidays in the peace of the English countryside. To aid them in their search they enlisted the help of a new friend, John Cross. George Lewes had first met John Cross's widowed mother when on a walking trip in 1867. When Mrs Cross had heard that the Leweses were in Rome three years later, she took the liberty of calling on them with her son, a broker in the city. Lewes made some financial investments through John Cross and then asked him to search for a country property.

George Eliot was suffering with continued bouts of neuralgia at this time and would often be in agony, which meant her progress writing *Daniel Deronda* was slow. It was the only one of her novels set in the time in which she wrote it and, in its pages, she reveals that racism in the late-nineteenth century might be just as casual as it is today. The views of Gentiles towards Jews were openly hostile, or subtly so, but in either case, George Eliot reveals that feelings towards Judaism could be complex. Once Daniel discovers his true heritage, he is determined to continue the work of Mordecai, the Jew who has taught him so much about the Jewish religion, and find a true homeland for the Jewish people. In marrying Mirah, he is further consolidating his Jewish roots.

Restrictive society

Gwendolen, the antithesis of Mirah, is self-absorbed and chooses to idle away her time in fruitless pursuits such as gambling. She thrives on always having self-control, but when marriage to Grandcourt robs her of this, she is forced to re-evaluate her whole life. Grandcourt marries her in order to break her, believing she is his property to do with as he pleases. Only after Grandcourt's death does Gwendolen begin to learn the value of humility.

Throughout *Daniel Deronda*, George Eliot was able to examine some of her most important and perhaps mature themes, such as the suppression of women in unhappy marriages, religious intolerance, religious identity, and, once again, the impact a restrictive society can have on individuals. These were the themes that time and time again were proved to resonate with various readers, many of whom were also struggling to find their own place in society.

George Eliot did not finish *Daniel Deronda* until the summer of 1876, although John Blackwood went ahead and published the first instalment in February 1876, perhaps keen to please those readers eager for more from the writer of *Middlemarch*. The novel was well-received by many Jewish readers, who enjoyed the fact that their religion was being so openly discussed in such a positive way. Other readers felt the novel would have fared better if the religious element had been excluded completely, allowing George Eliot to focus instead on the story of Gwendolen Harleth.

After the publication of *Daniel Deronda*, personal matters began to overtake all else for George Eliot. Previous to the publication of her novel, she had been plagued by ill health but now, just when John Cross had found a suitable house, the Heights, in Haslemere, for the Leweses to escape to, Lewes's own health began to deteriorate quite significantly. The couple chose not to entertain very much when at the Heights, preferring to enjoy the peace and solitude of each other's company, but it became impossible to ignore the pain and discomfort Lewes was in. When they returned to the Priory, their doctor, Sir James Paget, was consulted, but it was clear that little could be done. George Henry Lewes died on 30 November 1878. He was buried at Highgate Cemetery on 3 December. George Eliot was unable to attend. She had lost the great love of her life.

Chapter Fourteen

In which the world loses one of its greatest writers

Those only can thoroughly feel the meaning of death
who know what is perfect love.

(*Life and Letters*)

George Eliot saw in the year 1879 alone and with only her grief for company. When she felt able, she spent the following months on finishing an incomplete manuscript of Lewes's – the fourth volume of *Problems of Life and Mind* – which he had been working on at the time of his death. She was also in the middle of completing her own set of essays, *Impressions of Theophrastus Such*, and was only able to do so because she believed Lewes would have expected her to complete her work in spite of her grief.

She did not see John Cross until February, and with his financial knowledge he was a great support when it came to putting business and financial matters in order. Throughout 1879, George Eliot came to rely upon him for guidance and advice, particularly as she often received requests for monetary support from less well-off relatives and friends. Bertie's widow Eliza was someone who often needed financial aid, and John Cross seemed able to know how best to handle such pleas for help. They were also drawn together by grief, as Cross had lost his own mother just days after Lewes had died, so he was able to share something of George Eliot's pain. Indeed, the pair became mutually dependent, both helping the other to face the world again, and taking an interest in the other's pastimes. In spite of their twenty-year age gap – George Eliot was 60 at the time of their flourishing relationship – they found their friendship turning to love. This might have surprised those who had known the Leweses well. After all, they had been inseparable for twenty-four years and risked everything to be together. But ultimately, in spite of her mental strength and intelligence, George Eliot was a woman who was happiest when supported by the love of another individual. Less than two years after the death of George Henry Lewes, John Cross proposed to her and she accepted. Only a few intimate friends were initially told about the wedding, which took place on 6 May 1880, at St George's, Hanover Square. Barbara Leigh Smith Bodichon and the Brays were both pleased that their friend had a chance of renewed happiness, and as George Eliot kept reinforcing, Lewes had been exceptionally fond of John Cross. Lewes's son Charles accepted the news with good grace and even walked his stepmother down the aisle. Some outsiders and members of the general public gave a mixed response to the wedding, calling into question George Eliot's love for Lewes if she was able to marry again so quickly.

Brother Isaac is pleased

One person who was pleased to hear her news was her brother Isaac. George Eliot wrote to him through the family solicitor, Mr Holbeche, in order to inform him of her happy news. Her real and legally binding marriage to the unmarried John Cross made his sister socially acceptable in Isaac's eyes, and so he broke his silence of over twenty years to write back and congratulate her:

> My Dear Sister,
> I have much pleasure in availing myself of the present opportunity to break the long silence which has existed between us, by offering our united and sincere congratulations to you and Mr Cross.

George Eliot received his letter with acceptance, glad to put behind her their acrimonious and painful parting of the ways, and in responding she proved she was willing once more to enter into a correspondence with her brother. However, the fact that she informed him of her marriage through his solicitor suggests their relationship was still marred by formality and past regret.

After their wedding, the new Mr and Mrs Cross spent a night in Dover before departing for a honeymoon touring France and Italy. All appeared well until the honeymoon incident in Venice, which has continued to baffle many. One evening in June after a day spent sightseeing, for no reason that can be accounted for, John Cross threw himself from the window of the bedroom he shared with his new wife. It is apparent that he intended to drown, as the window overlooked the Grand Canal, but he was saved by some gondoliers. Concerned, George Eliot sent for her husband's brother, Willie Cross, who arrived as quickly as he could. Rumours circulated and indeed continue to do so as to why such a newly-married man would try to commit suicide on his honeymoon. In her journal, George Eliot wrote only the briefest of entries regarding the arrival of doctors, but included nothing specific about her husband's motivations. Later, John Cross would claim that he felt physically ill from a lack of clean air, while the less-genteel at the time maintained that he preferred to jump rather than spend one more night with his 'ugly', much older wife. There were also rumours that Cross suffered from a mental illness and that his family history was tainted by suicide, but Cross was never again to repeat the suicide attempt and lived until he was 84. The book he wrote about his wife, *George Eliot's Life as Related in her Letters and Journals by her husband J W Cross* was published in three volumes by Blackwood in 1885, but it was heavily doctored and censored. Cross was careful to leave out any incidents which he believed portrayed his wife in a negative way, or contradicted long-held beliefs about her.

When Cross was once more back to full health, the honeymoon continued for a further two weeks before the couple returned to Britain. They spent the summer at the Heights, but it was not long before George Eliot's health began to deteriorate once more. This time, her kidneys appeared to be the problem. Before leaving for their honeymoon they had settled on a house in Cheyne Walk, Chelsea, as a permanent residence and were glad to be able to take possession of it at the beginning of December. But George Eliot's condition was beginning to decline. She was afflicted with a sore throat and her kidney infection showed no sign of abating. In fact, it grew gradually worse. She was in continual pain and collapsed in agony before losing consciousness. By 10.00 pm on the night of 22 December 1880, she was dead.

George Eliot was buried a week later next to George Henry Lewes in Highgate Cemetery. Her brother Isaac travelled from Coventry to attend her funeral, able at last to say his final goodbyes to the sister from whom he had been estranged for so long. She was put to rest, as she wanted, next to the man for whom she had relinquished so much. Ultimately, their relationship had enriched her life and brought her the love and joy she had always craved and deserved.

George Eliot is now considered to be one of the greatest writers, not just of the nineteenth century, but of any century. She left behind a legacy of great works, and as a formidable member of the classical canon, she will always be recognised as someone who was able to transcend time through her creation of unforgettable characters, and her discussion of themes that are as relevant today as they were 150 years ago. She will also be remembered as a woman of great strength, and as someone who had the courage to live the life she wanted at a time when society tried hard to forbid such transgressive behaviour.

Further Reading

For the Interested Reader

Below is a list of websites and books which readers may which to access in order to continue their study of George Eliot further.

Primary materials

These websites are useful for finding contemporary reviews of George Eliot's novels:
www.britishnewspaperarchive.co.uk
www.nationalarchives.gov.uk
www.bl.uk

Non-fiction of the time

Beeton, I., *Book of Household Management,* Orion Books (London, 2007 reprint)
Cross, J., *George Eliot's Life as Related in her Letters and Journals by her husband J W Cross*, The Project Gutenberg (e-book www. gutenberg.org)
Eliot, G., *Selected Essays, Poems, and Other Writings*, Penguin Classics (London, 1990 reprint)

Fiction

Barrett Browning, E., *Aurora Leigh*, Norton Critical Editions (New York, 1995)
Brontë, C., *Jane Eyre*, Oxford World's Classics (Oxford, 2008)

Dickens, D., *David Copperfield*, Penguin Classics (London, 2004)

Eliot, G., *Adam Bede,* Wordsworth Classics (Hertfordshire, 2003)

Eliot, G., *Daniel Deronda,* Penguin Classics (London, 1986)

Eliot, G., *Felix Holt: The Radical*, Penguin Classics (London, 1995)

Eliot, G., *Middlemarch,* Penguin Classics (London, 1994)

Eliot, G., *Romola,* Penguin Classics (London, 2005)

Eliot, G., *Scenes of Clerical Life,* The Penguin English Library (London, 1973)

Eliot, G., *Silas Marner*, The Millennium Library (London, 2000)

Eliot, G., *The Lifted Veil and Brother Jacob*, Oxford World's Classics (Oxford, 2009)

Eliot, G., *The Mill on the Floss*, Penguin Classics (London, 2003)

Modern non-fiction

Adams, K., *Those Of Us Who Loved Her*, The George Eliot Fellowship (Warwick, 1980)

Gordon, L., *Outsiders*, Virago (London, 2017)

Hughes, K., *George Eliot, The Last Victorian*, Fourth Estate (London, 1998)

Laski, M., *George Eliot*, Thames and Hudson (London, 1987)

Index

Anglicans, 15, 53
Antwerp, 127-128
Arbury Hall, 17, 35, 36, 39-40,
  43, 59, 63
Astley, 17-18

Baptists, 57
Barrett Browning, Elizabeth, 23,
  24-26
  Aurora Leigh, 24-28
Beeton, Isabella, 114, 115, 175
  Mrs Beeton's Book of
    Household Management,
    114, 175
Belgium, 127, 130, 180
Belloc, Bessie Raynor (née
  Raynor Parkes), 136, 137-138,
  140, 142
Bentham, Jeremy, 100
Bern, 172
Bird Grove, Coventry, 61-62, 79
Blackwood, John, 161-162,
  163, 174, 175, 177, 178, 180,
  187, 190
Blackwood's Magazine, 161, 162
Bodichon, Barbara (née Leigh
  Smith), 137, 140, 142, 182, 189
Brabant, Dr Robert, 74-75, 82,
  90, 91, 128

Bray, Cara (Caroline, née
  Hennell), 63, 64, 71-73, 74, 78,
  84, 85, 86, 114, 118, 125, 134,
  154, 155
Bray, Charles, 63-66, 72-73,
  76, 114, 127, 136, 153, 154,
  155, 173
Brontë, Anne, 11, 23, 111
  The Tenant of Wildfell Hall, 11
Brontë, Charlotte, 28, 30-31,
  104-105, 111, 112, 142
  Jane Eyre, 28, 30-31,
    103-105, 112
Brontë, Emily, 111
Browning, Robert, 185
Burdett-Coutts, Angela, 120
Burlington Arcade, London,
  110, 118

Cambridge Street, Hyde Park
  Square (Number 21), 125, 127
Chapman, John, 77, 82, 83-84,
  97, 98-103, 106, 108, 126, 135,
  160, 170
Chapman, Susanna, 98, 101-103
Cheyne Walk, Chelsea, 190
cholera, 92-93
Christian Evangelicalism, 49,
  50-51

Clarence Row, East Sheen
(Number 7), 135
Clarke, Chrissey (née Evans), 7,
45, 48, 49, 58, 61, 81, 82, 86,
91, 96-97, 165, 171
Clarke, Dr Edward, 49, 61, 96, 97
Cologne, 128
Cornhill Magazine, The, 178
cooperative movement, 63
Coventry, 48, 56, 59, 61-63, 66, 68,
71, 76, 78, 85, 86, 91, 103, 190
Coventry Herald, The, 83
Cross, John Walter, 167, 186, 187,
188-190

D'Albert Durade, François, 8,
89-91
dame schools, 47-48
Defoe, Daniel, 60
Dickens, Charles, 111, 112, 114,
120, 162-164
David Copperfield, 120-122
Dover, 79, 132-134, 189

Eliot, George,
Adam Bede, 122, 147-148,
149-150, 164, 167-170, 176,
181, 185
birth (as Mary Ann Evans), 35
Brother and Sister Sonnets,
40-41, 181
childhood, 35-49
Daniel Deronda, 3, 4, 21, 50,
69, 186-187
death, 190
education, 47-49, 50, 56-57, 59
Felix Holt, The Radical, 98,
148, 179-181, 183

Feuerbach, *The Essence of
Christianity* (Translation),
126, 130
*Impressions of Theophrastus
Such*, 35, 188
Lifted Veil, The, 171
marriage, 189
Middlemarch, 1, 3, 22, 78,
131, 137, 142-147, 172,
183-185, 187
Mill on the Floss, The, 2, 3, 7,
32, 42-44, 45-47, 88, 96-97,
124, 151, 171, 173-174
non-fiction writing and editing,
28-29, 34, 83, 99-100, 103,
105-107, 131, 135, 139-142,
155, 157, 160
relationship with George Henry
Lewes, 41, 110-111, 118,
122-123, 124, 126-135,
137-139, 153-167, 170-171,
172-175, 176-182, 183-187
religion, 13-14, 16-17, 50-51,
54-55, 57, 60, 62-63, 65,
66-72, 83, 99-100
Romola, 147, 176-178, 180
Scenes of Clerical Life, 8, 9,
18, 36, 51, 160-162, 164,
167, 170
Silas Marner, 14-17, 39, 53-55,
62, 70-71, 148, 172, 175, 176
Silly Novels by Lady Novelists,
139-142
Spanish Gypsy, The, 181
Spinoza, *Ethics,* (Translation),
131, 133
Strauss, *The Life of Jesus*
(Translation), 74

translations, 74, 76-77, 123, 126, 130, 131-132, 133, 134

Emerson, Ralph Waldo, 64

English Women's Journal, The, 138

Evans, Christiana, 35, 45, 80

Evans, Fanny, 45, 81, 86

Evans, Isaac, 39, 40-41, 45, 47, 48, 60-61, 69, 78, 81, 86, 96, 164-167, 189, 190

Evans, Robert, 14, 17, 20, 35, 38, 42, 45, 51, 58, 59, 61-63, 66, 68-70, 78-79, 81, 84, 168

Evans, Robert (son of Robert Evans), 45, 81

Evans, Thomas, 45

Evans, William, 45

Factory Act (1833), 112

First Reform Act (1832), 180

Florence, 176

Foleshill, Coventry, 61, 63, 66, 67, 68-69

Frankfurt, 128

Franklin, Mary and Rebecca, 56-58, 70

Froude, James, 82-84
The Nemesis of Faith, 82-83

Gaskell, Elizabeth, 142

Geneva, 85-88, 91, 129

Gladstone, William, 22

Gliddon, Katherine, 116

Goethe, 123, 128, 130, 132, 133, 166

Gothic architecture, 35

Gothic Revival, 35

Grand Canal, the, Venice, 190

Grand Tour, the, 85

Griff House, Nuneaton, 9, 19-20, 38, 40-42, 45, 46-48, 50, 58, 59, 61, 62, 69

Guard, Pippa, 2, 3

Hardy, Thomas, 23

Heights, The, Haslemere, 187, 190

Hennell, Charles, 63, 74, 91
An Inquiry into the Origins of Christianity, 62-63, 74

Hennell, Rufa, (Elizabeth Rebecca, née Brabant), 74-75, 136

Hennell, Sara, 76-77, 134, 154-155, 175, 178

Highgate Cemetery, 187, 190

Holbeche, Vincent, 165, 189

Holly Lodge, Wandsworth, 171, 173

Holy Trinity Church, Coventry, 62, 66

Hunt, Thornton Leigh, 116

Huxley, T H, 100, 155

Ilfracombe, 155-157, 159

Industrial Revolution, 38, 62, 63-64, 175

Isle of Wight, 79, 178

James, Henry, 7

Jervis, Swynfen, 113, 116

Jewish heritage, 186

Jones, Reverend John Edmund, 51

Keats, John, 36
Isabella, or *The Pot of Basil*, 36

Lathom's, Miss (School for Girls), 4, 45, 48
Leader, The, 116, 130, 135, 155
Letts, John, 6
Lewes, Agnes (née Jervis), 113-114, 115-118, 130, 132, 172
Lewes, Charles, 172-173, 182, 189
Lewes, George Henry, 41, 104, 110-118, 122-123, 124, 126-128, 130-133, 135-136, 138-139, 147, 153-155, 157-162, 164-167, 170-173, 175-180, 182, 185-187, 188-189, 190
Lewes, Herbert (Bertie), 172-173, 182
Lewes, Thornton, (Thornie) 113, 172-173, 182
Lewis, Maria, 50, 56, 66
Liszt, Franz, 129-130
London, 7, 22, 61, 77, 91, 92-93, 95, 97, 98, 101, 108, 110, 111, 127, 128, 132, 133, 134, 145, 154, 155, 165, 170, 171
Lowood Institution, 111
Lynn, Eliza, 75

Mackay, Robert, 99-100
The Progress of the Intellect, 99-100
Martineau, Harriet, 71, 142

Nantglyn School, 56-57
Natal, 182
Necessitarianism, 64-65
Newdegate Square, Nuneaton, 6
Newdigate family, 17, 35, 39, 40
Newdigate, Francis Parker, 38
Newdigate, Sir Roger, 35

New Testament, 76, 83
Noel, Edward, 73
Nuneaton, 4-6, 9, 13, 19, 38, 49, 50-51, 81

Owen, Robert, 63-64

Paget, Sir James, 187
Park Shot, Richmond, 153
Parkes, Joseph, 76-77, 138
Patmore, Coventry, 23-24
The Angel in the House, 23-24, 25
Pears, Abijah, 63
Pears, Elizabeth (née Hennell), 63
Priory, The, St John's Wood, 7, 22, 179, 182, 185, 187

Queen Victoria (and her children), 185

Radicalism, 63
Rawlins, Sarah, 60
religious identity, 187
religious intolerance, 186
Rosehill, 64, 71-75, 79, 84, 91, 99, 103, 134, 153, 155
Rossetti, Christina, 119
Cousin Kate, 119-120
Rousseau, Jean-Jacques, 85
Rubens, Paul, 127
The Descent of the Cross and *Elevation of the Cross*, 127-128

Saturday Review, The, 174, 180
Scott, Sir Walter, 60, 79, 81
self-education, 59, 111

Shakespeare, William, 60, 136
  Passionate Pilgrim, The, 133
  Two Gentlemen of Verona, 133
  Venus and Adonis, 132
Smith, George (Smith, Elder and Co), 103, 177-178, 180
Spectator, The, 184
Spencer, Herbert, 100, 107-110, 111, 170
Steane, Hannah, 73
Stephen, Leslie, 22
Strand, The (Number 142), 98, 102-103, 118, 125
Swansea, 4, 5, 20, 159

Tenby, 159-160
Tennyson, Alfred Lord, 23, 29-30
  The Princess, 29-30

textile heritage, 62
Tilley, Elisabeth, 64, 102
Transcendentalism, 64
Trollope, Anthony, 176
Trollope, Thomas, 176

Urania Cottage, 120

Venice, 190

Wallington, Mrs, 49-50, 56
Weimar, 127-128, 135
Westminster Review, 28, 97, 99-100, 102, 103, 105-106, 107, 110, 118, 135, 139, 155, 160
Woolf, Virginia, 22